Harvest

The True Story of Alien Abduction

Harvest

The True Story of Alien Abduction

G.L. Davies

6TH
BOOKS

Winchester, UK
Washington, USA

JOHN HUNT PUBLISHING

First published by Sixth Books, 2020
Sixth Books is an imprint of John Hunt Publishing Ltd., No. 3 East St., Alresford,
Hampshire SO24 9EE, UK
office@jhpbooks.com
www.johnhuntpublishing.com
www.6th-books.com

For distributor details and how to order please visit the 'Ordering' section on our website.

Text copyright: G.L. Davies 2019

ISBN: 978 1 78904 385 3
978 1 78904 386 0 (ebook)
Library of Congress Control Number: 2019937321

A CIP catalogue record for this book is available from the British Library.

Design: Stuart Davies

UK: Printed and bound by CPI Group (UK) Ltd, Croydon, CR0 4YY
Printed in North America by CPI GPS partners

We operate a distinctive and ethical publishing philosophy in
all areas of our business, from our global network of authors to
production and worldwide distribution.

Contents

The G.L. Davies Interviews in Chronological Order

A most haunted house (included in Haunted: Horror of
Haverfordwest)
Ghost sex: The violation
Harvest: The true story of alien abduction
Haunted: Horror of Haverfordwest
(6th Books, ISBN: 978 1 78535 843 2)

Dedicated to the memory and work of Kevin Malek

Introduction

Two possibilities exist: Either we are alone in the Universe or we are not. Both are equally terrifying.
Arthur C. Clarke

Are we alone in the universe?

Before we begin our investigation into the terrifying ordeal that one woman from Pembrokeshire in West Wales endured (and she is possibly just one of many hundreds of thousands around the world) let's examine this question. It may, after all, help us understand her plight.

I don't know about you, but I enjoy looking up into the night sky and admiring the spray of cosmic majesty. Just tilt your neck on a clear night and endless possibilities and wonders can feed your imagination and soul. On the best nights we can see up to about 2,500 stars, roughly one hundred-millionth of those in our galaxy, sprinkled across a blanket of ebony.

We've been doing that for millennia, pondering the question of life in our cosmos. It is increasingly difficult today to believe it is exclusive to our planet. We know so much more than in past ages about the magnitude and scale of our universe – though scientists reckon that 95% of what the universe is made of is still unknown to us, and it may exist in multiple or infinite numbers of dimensions.

What we do know about the observable universe is staggering enough – it's estimated to be around 45.5 billion light years, with one light year approximately 10 trillion kilometres. Think of a pea in the Atlantic Ocean – that's the size of our solar system in relation to our galaxy. In relation to the size of the universe, our galaxy is again the size of a pea in the Atlantic. There are at least ten trillion planetary systems. Our planet is a mere submicroscopic speck in a colossal marvel of immeasurable possibilities.

How did we appear on this world? Are we a serendipitous fluke of creation, a lonely cosmic seed that might one day blossom and populate the galaxy? Or were we created by God? Evolution or divine creation?

There is also an increasingly popular third alternative – that we've been engineered. Has advanced alien life visited Earth and originated the human race?

Seventy-seven per cent of all Americans surveyed by the *National Geographic* believe that sophisticated alien life has visited the Earth. Fewer than ever before believe in a religious explanation of how we appeared on the planet. But are UFOs and the idea of intelligent aliens monitoring the lives of humans an illusion? Has there been a government cover-up, or is this just an imagined conspiracy?

There has been a huge amount of dedicated research on this, and great volumes written on this subject. Amazing accounts have captured the imagination of generations – the Roswell Incident, the Rendlesham Forest military account, the case of Billy Meier, the Betty and Barney Hill abduction, and many others. There have been reports of cattle mutilation, human harvesting, the Black Knight satellite, international space stations' images of strange craft cloaking and de-cloaking, flying saucers in Antarctica, colossal objects seen orbiting our sun – these are just a few of the thousands of cases reported in recent times. But these phenomena are more than a modern fiction; they have always been with us. They are woven into the fabric of our mythology, our religion, maybe even our history.

There is so much to ponder here. If we were engineered, then for what purpose? Are we the workforce of an advanced and ancient alien civilization? Are we to them merely cattle in a field, waiting to be culled? Perhaps we were merely created as a delicacy or aphrodisiac for an unsympathetic alien culture, or a race of cannon fodder bred for an intergalactic war soon to come? Are we the experiment of a creationist super being or is the Earth a soul factory, a place where souls are cultivated to journey to new worlds and inhabit new beings after the shell that we call a body dies?

The possibilities are endless. In the grand scheme of things though, does it really matter? All these theories may have little bearing on our modern lives. Regardless of how we became the race we are, we have to continue in our daily routines to survive. It is not the aliens that have to pay the bills, take the children to school or take out the bin bags.

Besides, if you believe that advanced alien life not only exists in the universe but regularly visits our small spinning blue globe, speckled with human life, what can you do about it? Sleep with a shotgun next to the bed or barricade yourself into your home?

I've written this book to help you find your own answers to these questions. And perhaps to find the most important one of all – are alien life forms likely to be friendly or hostile?

This is a serious, much-discussed issue. There is currently a debate on whether we should engage in METI (Messaging Extraterrestrial Intelligence) or simply SETI (Search for Extra-terrestrial Intelligence). Many say it's best not to broadcast our presence. Stephen Hawking, the best-known astrophysicist of the 20th century, warned, *"If aliens visit us, the outcome would be much as when Columbus landed in America, which didn't turn out well for the Native Americans."*

Even Carl Sagan (American cosmologist, science populariser and a general believer that any civilization advanced enough for interstellar travel would be altruistic rather than antagonistic) called the practice of METI, *"deeply unwise and immature,"* and recommended that: *"... the newest children in a strange and uncertain cosmos should listen quietly for a long time, patiently learning about the universe and comparing notes, before shouting into an unknown jungle that we do not understand."*

In a world of social networking, we invite people we barely know through a window into our world. But the idea that alien visitors may also be peering into our lives with an unknown agenda is more disturbing.

I was just ten years old when I began to ask these questions. I had grown up enjoying the Hollywood blockbusters from Stephen Spielberg like *E.T. the Extra-Terrestrial*, with its altruistic conservationist alien on his very human-like quest to simply go home and be with the beings he loves, and the benevolent alien emissaries in *Close Encounters of the Third Kind*. (It is interesting to note that during the White House screening of *E.T. the Extra-Terrestrial* President Ronald Reagan leaned over to director Stephen Spielberg, and quietly commented, *"You know, there aren't six people in this room who know how true this really is."*)

So my impression at a young age was that sophisticated life in the universe would be amiable, compassionate, gentle and treat us humans as equals, or at the very least give us a helping hand. Then one day in school that notion was crushed like a beetle under a steamroller. On a warm summer afternoon, the class all were huddled around our wonderful teacher. She was middle-aged, nurturing and passionate in her duty. She wanted to help the children she taught to have the best possible start in life.

She had read us such greats as *The Silver Sword* by Ian Serraillier, the classic tale of a journey through war-torn Europe, and the father-son relationship of *Danny the Champion of the World* by Roald Dahl. Those sunny Friday afternoons in the class were dreamy; my imagination would run wild, as my mind drifted like daisy seeds in a gentle breeze, from adventure to adventure, meeting all manner of marvellous characters.

Then she read to us a book called *The Uninvited* by Clive Harold. It was a story of a family entangled in a series of unearthly encounters. This was not E.T., the lovable, child-friendly brown alien with his plant pot, but malevolent and terrifying alien visitors that wreaked fear and pandemonium on a family.

Not only did this story appear to be true but it happened ten miles from the impregnable safety of my own home! To add to the ever-growing discomfort and vulnerability I felt during the reading, this terrifying account didn't happen in the murky and distant past but in the clear and magnified present. Not five years had passed since the invasion into the family's home had taken place. My daydreams turned into a nightmare. I was terrified, and to this day cannot fathom why Miss had chosen that book to read to us. Maybe in her own way she wanted to educate and prepare us for what was to come, but whatever her motives were I am now truly grateful for the introduction into this harrowing phenomenon. This was my first aware step into the unknown.

I went home that night with visions of aliens prowling the darkness, peering through windows as unsuspecting families settled in for the night in front of the TV, and of disembodied hands touching innocents while they slept, leaving horrendous burn marks on their flesh, as had been inflicted on that defenceless family in the book.

That night sleep escaped me, and I lay in the darkness of my room frightened and small. If the family's accounts of alien infringement were true, then nobody was safe from these extraterrestrial beings. Their superior technology and lack of regard for people made them the equivalent of a scientist experimenting on a rabbit or ape. I was appalled. I was vulnerable. I was very much troubled.

My father, sensing my apprehension, quietly knocked on my bedroom door. The door opened, and he stood there, a shadow engulfed by the breaching light from the landing. It was a reassuring silhouette. He came in and sat on the bed, and mentioned that I had told my grandmother of being upset by a book in school. I lay there and cried. I felt so scared yet so foolish. I believed that boys of my age were not supposed to cry.

Dad sighed and lifted me from the bed and hugged me. The most wonderful and reassuring hug you could imagine. He worked hard, putting in shifts at the local cheese factory, and despite his need for a hot bath and dinner had come in to comfort and reassure his frightened son.

He asked me if I had ever seen a ghost. I was taken aback by his inquiry. I believed I had. When I was four I had an imaginary friend who wore a top hat, a waistcoat and smoked a pipe. The odd thing was that he had been seen by countless people over many years, a well-known spirit who haunted the mill where we had lived. I had spoken to this ghostly man at length and found him to be kind and funny, little realising he no longer lived by the rules of our world. Though given that I was only four years old I make no claims as to the veracity of this experience.

"Did he harm you?" Dad asked. I replied in the negative.

"Do you remember when we saw that UFO?" he asked.

I recalled the time. It was when I was seven or eight years old, and my father and I were walking home down a dark (and notoriously haunted) country lane. We saw a large silent light drift up into the clouds. It was so bright that it illuminated the clouds beneath it. It then passed in front of us and vanished in a great silent white flash.

"Had we been hurt that night, had we been harmed?" he asked.

"No, but it scared me. I thought it was searching for someone, and when it found what it was looking for that person would never be seen ever again."

Dad put me back into bed and pulled the blankets over me.

"Gav, if ghosts and aliens do exist," he said, "doesn't that make the world exciting? It's the living who do the most harm, who will let you down and crush your dreams and make you unhappy."

He kissed me on the forehead and said I needed to sleep, and if I was still upset in the morning that he would go into school and talk to my teacher.

He closed my door and left. The room submerged back into darkness. This time I was no longer scared. My thoughts were aflame with ideas of discovery and adventure. I was stimulated to choose a path of investigation and enlightenment. The world had many dark secrets, but I had chosen a path to walk upon, to be a shining light.

I spent most of my years investigating and studying the paranormal. My first investigation at the age of eleven was into the ghost of a white lady said to haunt a ruined house nearby. Some young boys had been brought to tears by what they believed to be the figure of a woman in a torn and tattered dress running through the brambles. I quickly discovered how the power of suggestion and a white plastic bag fluttering in the brambles could morph into a real and terrifying ordeal. I had learnt my first lesson to never take anything at face value and to carefully sift information. I have spent most of my life absorbed in the subject and delighted that I have you, the reader, and many like you, keen to join me on my search.

In 2014, I followed up my first book *A most haunted house* (now included as a near twenty-year comprehensive paranormal account entitled *Haunted: Horror of Haverfordwest*) with a very polarizing and graphic account called *Ghost sex: The violation*.

The book was a true account of a local woman's unfathomable and relentless subjugation to paranormal physical and sexual abuse. Fifty shades of ghost it was not. Commercially successful, the book was read by thousands, but many had found the material difficult to stomach. I had spent many months with the victim as she revealed her terrifying testimonial and I, alone, dealt with the backlash that followed. The project had exhausted me to the extent that I thought long and hard about hanging up my paranormal hat and looking at other creative pursuits on less psychological and emotionally demanding subjects.

I had to admit that the book had taken its toll on me. During the time of writing it, I had suffered two failed relationships and felt my resolve slipping away. Had I delved too far into the darkness? Should I have given up this area of inquiry after my own catastrophic relationship with the home featured in *Haunted: Horror of Haverfordwest*? I had long contemplated ceasing my unhealthy pursuit of unearthing the paranormal ordeals of Pembrokeshire people.

A close friend believed that in my time immersed in the paranormal world perhaps something of a metaphysical and insidious nature had latched on to me, draining me. That might sound preposterous, but I did give the suggestion much thought. I asked for advice and guidance, and was offered a blessing, a cleansing of sorts to rid myself of the problem. Almost immediately after the ritual had taken place I found myself more contented, even elated. Was it psychosomatic? A placebo effect? Whichever, it worked. I believe we are all in need of positive mental and emotional reaffirmation from time to time, and this was just what the (witch) doctor had ordered.

I decided that I would explore a different paranormal avenue for my next project (though mid-investigation I was pulled back to the haunted house in Haverfordwest), one that was different from the hauntings of my first two books. I mulled over the idea and then a thought struck me. It was my very own eureka moment. I would delve into the UFO activity that plagued my county of Pembrokeshire, to research cases that had become known as the Welsh Triangle.

In 1977 a series of incredible events began to happen in the peaceful habitat of Pembrokeshire, which I am proud to call home, and its neighbouring counties. The area was inundated with reports of UFOs in the sky and on the ground, of silver-suited alien visitors, strange visits from bizarre and berserk beings with evident psychic powers, and even a herd of cattle teleported miles in seconds.

Was it all hysteria? The local paper the *Western Telegraph* did a superb job of reporting these incidents on a weekly basis. The archived reports showed that these were ordinary people witnessing extraordinary things. The area was plagued by these visitations over a five-year period. The material was abundant, and the witnesses still alive to speak to. I used my platforms to ask the local population if anyone was willing to help me in my research.

Of the many replies I received there was one from a lady in her mid-twenties. Being too young to have been there at the time I thought that perhaps she was speaking on behalf of an older relative or friend who were perhaps keen to speak but were concerned about my motives and first needed some reassurance on how I was presenting the story nearly forty years later.

I met, as I normally do, the young lady at the coffee shop on the side of the river in Haverfordwest. I'll call her Susan. I have changed her name, as I often do in my accounts, to protect her identity. Even good friends are hesitant to meet me at this coffee shop now for fear that passers-by who know of me will think I am interviewing a new witness for a current investigation.

The people I speak to are real enough. They believe they have had real encounters. They have to live and deal with the frightening reality of what has happened to them. I sift out those I believe are fantasists, or who seem to be in it for the money or fame. I keep those I believe generally want their identity protected. They are nervous of being thought mad. There are few self-help groups of any credible nature that they can approach for comfort and reassurance regarding supernatural and other-worldly events. By speaking to me they believe they can unshackle themselves from the fear. It's a cathartic process for them, a help in closure. They want to warn people that there is far more to the world than we are taught to understand. I do at times feel I absorb their pain, their mental suffering. I say after each series of interviews, this is going to be the last. I hope this will be the case now.

Of course many belittle and reject their accounts. Materialists might believe that we have all the answers to the mysteries of time and space, God and the universe, and all the intricacies of the human mind. I would just encourage you to read with an open mind, accepting that it's possible our current understanding is limited. After all, the Earth was once considered to be flat, with the sun circling it.

Susan was more nervous than most. I tried to reassure her that though I would make notes, nothing was being recorded and everything was private at this stage. Not a word would be written without her personal consent.

She sat there and stared at me. She was very beautiful with stunning sea-green eyes. Her face wore a gauntness of someone who carried too much burden on her shoulders for such a young age. Despite hiding her tall frame in a baggy hoody and joggers her body betrayed an elegance and grace. She was well spoken. Articulate and concise, each word was presented exactly as it should have been. She began to tell me something unexpected. This was not about the Welsh Triangle case from all those years ago. No, this was recent, something deeply sinister and contemporary. It was something that had happened to her.

She gave me no further detail but asked could we meet somewhere more secluded and private, inviting me to her home the following week. This young woman had something dark and terrible to tell me. She had experienced incredible and startling encounters, and she was ready to finally tell the world.

This was not another haunting... this was something different. This was something altogether new in my canon of investigation. This is the story of a young Pembrokeshire woman who believed she was the victim of advanced alien visitation and their inhuman designs.

Is this story true? Form your own judgement. I cannot say for sure. All I know is that the woman involved believes it to be so. What she has revealed to me is harrowing, a warning that something terrible is coming our way, with consequences for the entire world. If there is even a kernel of truth here then there is nothing any of us can do to save ourselves.

Sleep well!

G.L. Davies
January 2019

Ascendance

When you read this incredible story, do not be too sceptical: Somewhere in your own past, there may be some lost hour or strange recollection that means that you also have had this experience. Instead of shunning the darkness, we can face straight into it with an open mind. When we do that, the unknown changes. Fearful things become understandable and a truth is suggested. The enigmatic presence of the human mind winks back from the dark.
Whitley Strieber, *Communion*

Interviewing begins October 2014

Susan had asked me to come to her flat alone and not to divulge the address. She insisted it was not a subject to be discussed via the telephone or online, but face to face. That suited me; I prefer that as it allows me to detect the minute telltale signs of fabrication and deceit. Susan stressed that I should not mention a word about our discussions until she felt her story was ready to be published. It was vitally important to her nothing was lost in translation or abbreviated to fit a fashion more acceptable for those looking for entertainment. She wanted her story told as it was.

The building was easy to find as I had walked past it countless times in my life, though I had never, as far as I was concerned, seen or been aware of Susan before. In Haverfordwest it is easy for social circles to overlap and for new acquaintances to be made. It's a small town, formerly walled and fortified, that serves as the centre point for the county of Pembrokeshire. Small, narrow streets nestle along the River Cleddau with the High Street descending the steep hill like an artery, where other roads branch off like veins. Picturesque, it is filled with character and history, with a majestic ruined castle that has stood sentinel for so many centuries.

I waited outside Susan's building to be buzzed in. Susan had laid down stringent rules on how we were to conduct a series of interviews. I would be punctual and respectful. If I followed her precedent without question and she was satisfied, then another session would be set up until the account had been entirely recorded.

The buzzer went and I pushed open the heavy door. As it closed decisively behind me I was greeted by a mass of letters and junk mail on the floor. Many of them emblazoned with the big red lettering of DO NOT IGNORE and FINAL NOTICE, along with takeaway menus and leaflets proclaiming SALES NOW ON. The hallway smelled of stale cigarette smoke and the light flickered, giving the hallway a dispiriting countenance.

Susan was in a flat on one of the higher floors. I made my way up the stairs. The sound of my feet echoed as I took each step. On one floor I heard the frantic commentary of a horse race and further on up another the loud and energetic sounds of intimacy; another floor reeked of the pungent aroma of cannabis. I finally reached the fourth floor and passed several doors to reach hers. Each door was silent as I passed. The area around her door surprisingly smelt of incense and freshly-baked bread.

I gave a reserved tap on the door. The gloom of the corridor gave me a sense of foreboding. I found the entire building to be discouraging, and it filled my heart with cheerlessness. I was not my usual excited self on this investigation. This woman and her record that she claimed to have so far suppressed was unknown territory for a man of my experiences. She had informed me that she lived alone and that we would not be disturbed. The thought had crossed my mind several times that would it be inappropriate to meet a young woman of whom I had little knowledge in her own home. I was leaving myself open for any form of accusation. I had decided if her demeanour was agitated or strange that I would leave immediately; or if the material looked like it was going to be of a personal nature as it had with

Ghost sex: The violation, then I would say it was necessary to have a female investigator join us.

I heard a door chain being lifted, and as the door opened inwards I was blinded by refreshing and reassuring sunlight. In the brightness stood the silhouette of a tall figure. It was Susan. She hurriedly invited me in, and I was greeted with a well-kept and homely abode, unlike the one I expected in my mind's eye.

She was dressed in her hoody and joggers, which I would discover over time was her usual state of dress. The flat was airier than I had expected, with two large windows and a skylight. The aroma of patchouli filled the room and made it agreeable and relaxing, compared to the steps I'd walked up.

Her flat consisted of a friendly kitchenette strewn with tins of tea, glass jars of pasta and the like, and every conceivable space seemed to house a cooking utensil. The living area was intimate and orderly with a settee adorned with a bright throw weaved from burgundy and avocado coloured threads. I was a little taken aback by the poster-sized prints on the wall. One was the depiction of Adam and Eve in the Garden in Rogier van der Weyden's *Triptych piece of the redemption* and the other the stark contrast of Hans Memling's *Death*. A bookshelf upon inspection carried an eclectic mix of titles from Bulgakov's *The Master and Margarita* to Matheson's *I Am Legend*. The occupant of this home had a more sophisticated lifestyle than I had expected. On her coffee table was another pile of books, *The Diving-Bell and the Butterfly* by Jean-Dominique Bauby, *The God Delusion* by Richard Dawkins and Huxley's *The Doors of Perception*.

Were these clues to her mindset and thought process, fuelling her perception of a ghastly otherworldly experience? I stared at her in her casual attire. She held herself tight, her arms wrapped around her like a person struggling to find warmth, more anxious than anyone I have interviewed before or since. My instincts told me this was going to be a very different process than I had first anticipated.

She asked me if I would like tea. I gratefully asked for an Earl Grey and she went quietly about making it. She curtly told me there would be no milk and that she was a vegan. Her demeanour was unsure and a little unsettling despite the homely surroundings. I sensed that she was almost regretting her decision to speak to me. Now I was in her home and she had two choices. Speak to me or ask me to leave.

She handed me my Earl Grey and pointed at the settee for me to sit upon. She disappeared into a hallway and reappeared carrying a bright red beanbag chair and sat down opposite me. She asked if I minded if she smoked to which I replied it was her home and smoking would not cause me any offence. She offered me a handmade cigarette which I refused, having given up both smoking and alcohol several years previously. She looked at me a long time with those beautiful green eyes.

I broke the silence and asked her if she was sure this was what she wanted to do – and then immediately regretted it. I was anxious to hear her story. She took a deep drag on her cigarette and slowly nodded. The room was soon occupied with the wisps of smoke, like manifesting ghosts, and redolent of tobacco. She took a long inward breath and finally spoke. It was time.

This account will shock many of you. If true, this woman has endured something unfathomable to human understanding. This is not a typical account of UFOs and alien abduction – it goes so much further into a sinister and dark world, a world of mystifying imagery, excruciating levels of inhumane torture and absolute fear and dread.

Susan conducted herself well. She seemed intelligent and thoughtful. She chose her words carefully, as if she had rehearsed this telling a hundred times over in her mind. She was clearly educated. Where? I do not know. I know so little about this young woman. She is untraceable on social media and she has only left a faint imprint on the world. Her words, her voice were hypnotic. I have never heard one so captivating. Certain pronunciations created a tingle down my scalp and into my spine. Some of her descriptions, the imagery she presented were so vivid, they were like poetry. I had to be careful to concentrate on her every word – maybe I was dealing with someone highly functional within the confines of a mental health issue. Her behaviour, her attire, her flat – all suggested a personality with very contrasting elements.

Those of you accustomed to my previous publications will know what is to follow are the words of the witness. This is her story in her own words. Some details have been left out to preserve her anonymity.

My style of questioning is to extract detail, so I can bring you, the reader, into the story, so that you can connect with the people and the events. I have included her musings, spoken thoughts and opinions as she recounts her tale. I have removed my questioning from the published testimonial so that it flows in an unhindered fashion. I shall bookend each section with my thoughts and observations. I have been given full permission from the interviewee to publish this account.

I respectfully request that you, the reader, concentrate on Susan's testimonial, empathise with an ordeal that she perceives to be real, and then ask yourself – if this is true, then what would you do in her place? Are you prepared for your life to change?

Susan: Please do not take my coldness or bluntness personally. You must realise that we live in a very sceptical world. There are people out there that will ask a million questions all with the agenda of trying to scrutinize my story for a slip-up or a contradiction that they can cleverly leap on and accuse me of being a liar. I have spent over five years trying to make sense of all of this.

I have read much on the psyche and how various outside and internal factors can be held accountable for my experiences, but from all my research I have not found an answer that would explain such vivid and intense experiences. There will be many that easily dismiss anything that they cannot understand, but I believe that is because they are frightened. They are frightened of the truth that we have tried to hide behind religion and science.

I was once sceptical. I would even go further and say that my scepticism was based on apathy. I did not care for such fantasy of the paranormal. Ghosts, aliens and monsters were all created by a man trying to make sense of his world, to understand the sky and stars above and to control his fear of death. My life was deeply rooted in the material world.

What I could do was to make significant changes that were valuable to me and the life I desired. I had ambitions and achievements that I needed to fulfil. I believed that life is about hard work, dedication and about making the life you want to have. I had little regard for the affairs of others and what was happening in the world. I would sponsor a tiger for £3 a month and think I was a great human being, and sometimes on the news there would be an earthquake and I would think how sad it was, but I did nothing to help them. I thought that my feelings of sadness and pity were in their own way enough – hardly humanitarian of the year. Those people, those victims were thousands of miles away, and there was nothing I could do to change their circumstances. Only now do I understand their helplessness, how desolate and life-changing it can be.

We are such an arrogant species. We think so highly of our abilities, yet we understand so little of what is really happening to us. We butcher and consume animals, we even kill each other like we are no more than rats in a nest, and we destroy our natural world. I'm not some activist looking for an outlet so I can piously rant. I'm saying this because even as we do all this, we are unaware of something very dominant that treats us like we treat animals. We are a commodity to them in the same kind of way, but no human could ever imagine the abuse they inflict.

I believe I have witnessed and experienced experimentation

and unimaginable pain and terror at the hands of a race that are not human. I have seen other women too, women that these beings also have designs on. I want women like me to know that they are not safe. Those sharp pains behind their eyes, sudden losses of memory, inexplicable rashes, pains in their groin, dreams of flashes, of coldness and screams, are the physical results of unwanted visitors.

I dread every single night that they will come again for me, that whatever it is they want they will come back for it. Dawn brings reassurance, but then it's just a countdown to the inevitable darkness and it begins again. For over five years I have lived on the edge of fear. They will return, and I will be plucked like corn in a field that is ready to be harvested.

Seed

I looked, and I saw a windstorm coming out of the north – an immense cloud with flashing lightning and surrounded by brilliant light. The centre of the fire looked like glowing metal...
Ezekiel 1:4

Susan: Everything has a starting point. There may have been earlier incidents, maybe something happened to me during my childhood years, but nothing springs to mind. I am not aware that I ever had a paranormal experience or seen anything strange in the sky.

My family were all very ordinary. Nothing psychic about them – I never heard anyone discussing ghosts or aliens. We were not religious. We'd go to the occasional service, out of duty – my parents still do, I don't. I've cut myself off from my family, and anything to do with God – no God would ever allow these horrors. My family do not understand what I have been going through... what I *am* going through. I can't blame them. They are intelligent, professional people.

I'm not going to go into my background, my education, the area I grew up in. I want to remain anonymous... I will remain anonymous at all costs. Pembrokeshire is a small place. People can work out your identity from the smallest clue. They can be so dismissive, so cruel. Even if it were proven that I am mentally ill it wouldn't stop their abuse. This is what worries me, not so much that they will hound me but how lacking in sensitivity they are. They're like the bullies in the school playground. Bullies who hide their own insecurities and take shots at people they feel are weaker than them.

I admit, I'm no saint myself. If I could trade my life for theirs then I would. Happily. I'd do anything to get back to before that night and have the life I wanted. Is that wrong of me? People who hear this can decide for themselves once they have the full facts.

I'll start my story the night I think it all began.

It was November, over five years ago, when I guess they first took an interest in me. I was staying with some friends. One of their parents had a farmhouse in the middle of the county. They were away on holiday. My friend said to come over, we would invite a couple of the other girls too. It would be just the four of us and a dog. She had a lovely dog, a boxer called Lennie that I was very fond of.

It was an idyllic, peaceful place. The plan was pyjamas, movies and a few bottles of Rioja. We were all studying in Carmarthenshire and working to very similar goals. I had known one of the girls, I'll call her Sian, since school, and the other two, Wendy and Karen, were on the same course as us. They were wonderful friends. I miss them all so much. I've got no contact with them now, that's how strained things became. They think I'm just a mentally ill weirdo. You've no idea how painful it is to see them succeed in life, while I've hidden away here – I try and keep civilized with pots and pans, cookbooks, routines, but it's difficult.

It had been a lovely evening. We were very career-minded and talked about the paths we had chosen and what we hoped to achieve. Soon our professional talk changed as the wine flowed and we started discussing relationships. Sian said we should call some local guys we knew that had asked us out to the pub with them earlier in the day. She messaged one of the guys to come over and bring the others, and to also bring some more alcohol. It was all so much fun. We were excited. We were all in our early twenties, free and single and letting our hair down. We studied hard and it was time for fun. Don't misinterpret this – we didn't want one-night stands, just company.

I went up to the loo. I remember it vividly as Wendy had just said something rude about one of the boys and I was giggling as

I went up the stairs to the bathroom.

The farmhouse was an old stone building. There was a wonderfully large living room with oak beams and a great old fireplace that we were burning logs on. The staircase was narrow leading up to the three bedrooms. The farmhouse was off a quiet road down a long bumpy track. The track was probably about a half a mile from the main road and descended quite steeply. The house nestled down in the fields of the valley and was circled by a row of trees and a small stone brick wall. There was another building that used to be a barn but had been converted into a garage with a nice guest apartment above, that was occasionally let out to holidaymakers in the summer. I had shotgunned the apartment on my arrival, and had bagged Lennie to be my guard dog and companion.

The bathroom had a low frosted window with a wooden sill and faced out towards the descending track. Above was a skylight. As I sat there chuckling I saw what I thought were the headlights of a car driving down the track. There was no way though that the guys had got there that quick, as they were a good thirty minutes away and Sian had only called them in the last five. I thought that it was obviously someone else visiting, or they'd taken the wrong turn. Once you are on the track there was nowhere to turn, and reversing back around the bends would be difficult, not that I ever did such a thing. I expected to hear Lennie start barking loudly to herald the arrival of visitors.

The lights continued down very slowly. I leant forward so I could see more through the frosted pane. Then they stopped. I thought the driver must have realised they had taken the wrong turn and was considering what they were to do. You must remember that this has taken twenty seconds at the most from the time I first saw the lights coming down the track to seeing them stop.

Suddenly the lights on the car went off, as did the bathroom light, and I was sat there in the pitch black. There was no light from outside and no light from under the bathroom door from the landing. I heard the girls shouting downstairs and Lennie barking, and I thought the power must have gone throughout the whole house. I felt around for the toilet paper when I was bathed in a bright white light from above. I looked up and the light was fierce, coming in through the skylight. There was no sound and I had to look at the light through the gaps of my fingers. I closed my eyes, but it was as if the brightness had left an imprint on my retinas. I could still see it.

I felt nothing of consequence, I was just a bit confused. Perhaps it was a helicopter. You often see them in the county, police ones, or search and rescue, or one of those red ones that checks the power lines. I thought, can they see me sitting on the loo? I thought how embarrassing it would be to see me like that in my pyjamas with my arse hanging out.

The bright light went out. It didn't drift away or diminish but simply went. One minute I was bathed in white light, the next I was sat in the darkness again. I was perplexed and then the bathroom light came back on and I heard cheering downstairs. I realised the power had come back on throughout the house.

I went back downstairs, and Sian hugged me and asked if I was OK. Wendy and Karen were laughing, imagining me sat on the loo in the dark all alone. They had piled wood on the fire. The room was warm, and the fire was high, casting flickering shadows on the stone walls. I remember the shadows intensely as they made me feel worried like they were spirits dancing, conjured by a tribal ritual.

Sian said I had been ages. I said I had not; I had been no more than five minutes. She said I had been up there for more like fifteen. I went to check my mobile phone and it was dead. I had to hold the on button for it to reboot and start up again. I had been gone ten minutes, but I thought it did not feel that long but, in the commotion, I probably lost track of time. I asked the girls if any of them had seen the light coming down the drive and then over the house. None of them had. Sian said that maybe it was the security light on the barn. I thought no, this was a car coming down the drive and then a light hovered on top of the house. None of them had seen it but they said that in the living room the thick heavy curtains had been drawn and during the power cut they had gone about busying with building up the fire and the lighting of candles.

I was not overly concerned. My rational thought was that maybe two incidents had simultaneously happened. One of these was a car was lost on the track, and the second an aircraft like a helicopter had passed over the farmhouse. If the power had gone then maybe it was the power line helicopter looking for a fault, and the car was maintenance men looking to fix it. It explained a lot and there was nothing to spend any more time thinking about. However, I did open the front door to see if there was a car on the track and I could see nothing but the stars dotted in the sky. I remember this all so vividly like I am there. I close my eyes and I can see everything as it was that night.

Back inside I soon put the episode behind me, and we drank and awaited the arrival of the boys. It was about ten minutes later that everyone realised that their mobile phones had powered off and needed rebooting and turning back on. When Sian's phone came back on, she received a text from the guy she had messaged, which said they would not be able to make it as their car had broken down outside the town they had just left. I do not think what happened at the farmhouse and the car breaking down are related at all. I guess that was purely coincidental. They had broken down nearly ten miles away and if the light been responsible for cars breaking down I am sure there would have been an epidemic of them.

We drank and laughed and listened to music. The fire got low and the living room started to get cold. We had drunk quite a bit. Wendy started dropping off and we all decided it was time for bed. It must have been around 2am when we called it a night. Sian tried to convince me to stay in and sleep in her parents' double bed with her as it was cold outside, and she was not fussed with the idea of me walking outside to the barn. I reassured her, telling her that Lennie would look after me. I had a secret agenda too. I wanted to have a smoke. I kept my smoking secret as I did not think it was a good habit to have in the profession I was studying to enter, besides I did not want my parents knowing. Now I smoke all the time; there are far worse things to worry about than cancer.

I said my goodbyes and laughed at Karen trying to help Wendy up the stairs and to bed. Sian gave me a long hug and begged me to stay inside. She said I was too stubborn but she was too tired to argue, and gave me the front door key in case I needed to come back in.

I left the farmhouse with Lennie on his lead. He had happily strolled beside me. It was so chilly that night. Being in a valley the temperature was cold. The farmhouse night light was on behind me. It only took twenty seconds, if that, to walk to the barn. I never felt threatened out there, never did. I never had a fear of nature. If I close my eyes now, I can see and feel it all so vividly. I could hear an owl far off in the distance and the tinkle of the stream that ran behind the barn. I got to the barn and opened the door. There was a small hallway. To the left was a door to the garage and then a flight of wooden stairs leading upwards. I walked up and opened the apartment door. It was nice and warm in there after being out in the night. The apartment was open plan with a kitchen, living area and a dining area. Tucked in the corner behind a wood-panelled wall about five feet tall was a double bed with a heavy duvet. At the opposite corner above the stairs was a small toilet with a shower. Like the farmhouse, the windows were very low but much taller, and there were around half a dozen skylights. It was amazing in there; the work that had been put into it was superb.

Lennie had jumped straight on to the bed, and I went back

downstairs as he lay down. The night light on the farmhouse had gone out, and I stood there and smoked and looked at the stars. The door behind me was ajar and let out a sliver of light and it was so peaceful. I still remember shivering with the cold and it did make me recall the incident earlier in the bathroom. That feeling made me feel uneasy, so I quickly finished my cigarette and headed back in. I locked the door on the way up. I remember doing this as I wondered if it was necessary. I thought though that whoever was on the track driving down could still be out there or the lads that were supposed to come over might decide to come and play a practical joke on us later in the night.

I went upstairs back in the warmth of the apartment. I used the loo and poured myself a pint of water and placed it beside the bed. Lennie had his face on his paws half asleep. I got into bed; the duvet was heavy and reassuring. The clock next to the bed if I recall correctly said 02.15 or thereabout. I turned off the lamp and lay there in the dark. Lennie was breathing heavily, and with a combination of wine and tiredness I dropped off.

That night I had a terrible dream. Or what I thought was a dream.

I woke up and the alarm clock showed 03.18 – I remember that time like it's tattooed on my brain – and then it flickered off. I felt as if there was someone moving around the room in the darkness. I could feel Lennie lying heavily on the bed and heard him breathing deeply still.

You can sense when someone is there. I was certain there was someone stood there in the darkness. I thought it might have been Sian, though I should have heard her unlock the front door and make her way up. I sat up a little and peered around. There seemed nothing there, but I could sense it. The hairs stood up on my neck and arms, and a cold feeling ran down my chest to the pit of my stomach. I had to be dreaming, right?

By the end of the bed, I thought I could make out something moving. There was something small. I thought it was child stood there. I could barely make out a small slender figure maybe three feet tall. It was just a dark silhouette. It was staring at me lying in the bed.

I panicked and was about to sit up when the entire room was filled with a bright white light. There were six thick bright columns of light pouring through the skylight and they quickly merged into one. It was the same intense light I had seen in the bathroom. Lennie barked and jumped off the bed. I could not move. I was propped up on one elbow shielding my eyes with my other hand. I heard something crash. The light quickly disappeared, and I was back in the darkness. I prayed Sian and the girls would hear and run over. I decided to just make a run for the door and get out. Lennie was growling ferociously in the darkness and things were being knocked over. I felt like my retinas had been burned and I could not make anything out. The pain in my head was so intense.

There was a blue smoky flash and I saw the room illuminated for a second. Like someone had taken a picture. I saw the outline of a dog, of Lennie attacking a tall black skinny figure. There was another blue flash and a high-pitched ringing, and I heard the howl of pain, an inhuman scream. Another flash and I saw Lennie crumpled into a heap on the floor. He was still and silent. Another flash and Lennie was nowhere to be seen.

Another blue flash and I saw a black featureless face mere inches from mine. I screamed.

I woke up with such a panic. I bolted upright. The clock showed 07.44. My head hurt so much. I had a terrible pain behind my right eye, like a migraine. I reached out for the water and it was not there. I peered over the side of the bed and the glass was broken on the floor. I presumed I had knocked it over during my nightmare. I went to sit up, but I had terrible cramping pains in my stomach. I had a sharp piercing pain in my back, it was like period pain but so much more intense. I knew I had drunk the night before, but this was not a hangover. I was in severe pain.

I looked around the room. I tried to orientate myself. The room looked as it did when I went to bed. Lennie was not on the bed, so I called for him. I thought that maybe during my night terror I had distressed him, and he had found a peaceful place to lie.

It took me a while to get out of bed. When I got to my feet I quickly hobbled to the toilet and I vomited. I felt horrendous. It was when I went to wipe my face that I saw I'd had a nosebleed in the night and there was dried blood around my nostrils and on my upper lip. I washed my face and hands and slowly made my way into the apartment. I could not see Lennie anywhere. I opened the top door and looked down the stairs, and still, he was not there. I thought that maybe Sian has taken him out; maybe she had gotten up early, popped over to the barn and taken him for a walk or to feed him.

It took me a good half an hour to collect myself and then make my way to the farmhouse. It was a cold morning with a mist on the surrounding hillocks. Thinking about how cold and grey it was still chills me to this day. The memory is incredibly depressing.

I used the front door key to make my way into the farmhouse. I expected Lennie to bark and jump all over me and the girls to be nursing their hangovers with tea and toast. The downstairs was quiet and still. I made my way slowly upstairs. Both Wendy and Karen were asleep in their respective rooms and Sian was face down in her parents' bed asleep. I walked over to her and lay beside her on the bed. She stirred and croakily asked what time it was, and I had told her. She turned and faced me and asked how I slept. I told her I had an awful dream, and she said it was probably because the power cut had been playing on my mind mixed with the wine. I asked her if she had been over to let Lennie out and she sat up and said no. She asked had I let him out or had I forgotten to lock the front door. I told her I had brought him into the barn and I had locked the door and he was on the bed when I went to sleep. She looked at me puzzled and she said we would go and look for him. We woke the others and the four of us went looking for him.

We never found Lennie. We never saw him again.

Watcher

Statistically, it's a certainty there are hugely advanced civilizations, intelligences, life forms out there. I believe they're so advanced they're even doing interstellar travel. I believe it's possible they even came here.

Astronaut Story Musgrave

Susan sat before me with a look of total melancholy. Deep down she bore the brunt of the blame for what happened that night. I asked myself if she was to blame for the disappearance of the family pet. Had she, in fact, drunk too much that night or had forgotten to lock the door, or a combination of both? It's easy to make those kinds of mistakes. But she was adamant in her point that the door was locked from the inside. Was this verbal reinforcement merely a mechanism to cope with her guilt?

I am no stranger to accounts of the unusual, and I found the sequence of events involving the dog, the flashes of light, a small dark creature, taller bandy ones and a faceless visitor to be quite unnerving. If this was not a dream, then had the dog been incapacitated or killed while faithfully trying to protect a family friend? But from what?

The dreamlike sequence and the light in the bathroom seemed too similar to be coincidental. Had a real experience in the evening in the bathroom conjured up a vivid nightmare? Just what had been behind that light on that dark and lonely track and the bright light from above? I needed to find out more from this woman. Maybe she had a medical condition that she was withholding from me or one she was unaware of.

I am not medically qualified to make assumptions, but as an investigator, I have a duty of care to my client, so if necessary I will advise professional help. Sadly, in some cases, I have had to contact said professionals to save a person from self-harm or harm to others. It is a situation I do not relish being in but is a necessary evil in my line of work.

Her story so far was detailed and brought many questions to my mind. I needed to probe further as we had only uncovered the tip of a very cold and dark iceberg. To all intents and purposes at this stage of the interviews, Susan appeared to be rational and balanced in her recounting. Her tone of voice, her body language and her micro expressions gave no hint of deceit. I knew that this story was going to become far more extraordinary and alarming. She did not disappoint. The interview continued.

Susan: I know you are thinking that I had lost Lennie, but I promise you that I did lock the door and I did see him with me in the apartment. Sian was deeply upset. They searched for days and found nothing. He was in good health, six or seven years old, and was not prone to wandering off. He was part of the family and every time I heard Sian say *not to worry, it wasn't my fault, he would turn up* I could hear the edge in her voice. She was heartbroken and deep down I knew she blamed me. Her silly friend got drunk and forgot to lock the door, and the dog escaped and now he had gone.

None of the neighbouring farms or houses had seen anything of Lennie. The police were involved, and kennels and local vets called. No one had seen him. Sian called the council to see if any dogs fitting his description had been collected as roadkill.

When her parents got back from holiday they were clearly also upset. The mother felt like they had lost a family member and grieved accordingly. I apologised to the parents and the mother sternly asked me why I hadn't just stayed in the house with the other girls. Sian was scolded for not acting more responsibly. It was no one's fault as far as I was concerned but an angry glare from Sian's mother told me better than to voice my argument.

I was never invited to the house again.

I still saw Sian and the others in college, but it was not the same. There was a divide between us. I wish I could just admit it was my fault, and take the blame and face the brunt of her anger but I had nothing to confess. As I continue with this story, I think what happened to Lennie will become more evident and that is what breaks my heart.

The days after Lennie went missing were awful. I felt incredibly ill. I had several nosebleeds, and the pain behind my eye was agonizing. Sian thought it was a hangover from the imaginary huge amount of wine I had drunk. I suffered terribly with diarrhoea and pains in my stomach after that night. I felt like I was in the grip of some terrible drug. Nothing seemed real. I was walking in a grey world shrouded in a cold mist, depressed and distraught.

I was not prone to feeling low back then. In general, I would say that I was a positive and focused person, but now I just didn't feel right in myself. Some people might think "it's only a dog" but it was more than that. I felt I had let my best friend down and hurt her family, and I didn't even know how I had managed it. I had no clue to what was behind the light I had seen above the house, and the dream in the apartment still haunted me. I was almost too scared to go to sleep. I checked in with the doctor, and he said I was run-down and had an iron deficiency. He prescribed a tonic and a change in diet. It did nothing to help.

At the time I was living at my aunt's house. She worked nights and I felt lonely after the events at the farmhouse and scared when she was not there. It was quite irrational. There was a guy I had been seeing on and off, and I asked him over a few times. We had been friends in school and things had developed after a night out. Nothing serious but it is nice to have the option of company, something I have now switched off from completely. He saw the invitation as much more, but I merely needed him to be there with me. So much for woman's empowerment, hey? I used the excuse of my period to keep his advances at bay. I just felt so alone. Now that I really am alone, I have gotten used to it.

I like cooking. I buy recipe books and kitchen utensils, though I have no one to dine with. I read constantly, it is my escape and company all in one. I treat each day as if it's my last supper, the last supper set for one. It sounds a little sad that a woman in her twenties behaves this way. I don't feel the need to make any friends. I can't make friends. The circumstances around my life will only get them hurt. What will happen to you, Mr Davies? I wonder?

I told this guy I was stressed and told him in part what had happened at Sian's. Let's call him Adrian. It will save me having to refer to him as that guy. Adrian was nice enough but was a little immature. They say whatever a guy's age is to take away ten years and that is his true age, which would have made him a teenage boy. He was quite charming in his own way but because he could drive, work and have sex he thought he was a mature and considerate man. He rarely paid any interest in what I had to say but occasionally he would surprise me. We were chalk and cheese in terms of our mentality and our goals in life, but we had got on since I had met him in school.

A few days, it was the third day, after the disappearance of Lennie, Adrian suggested we go for a drive and he would treat me to some food at a fast food restaurant in Pembroke Dock. Let's just say we dined under the golden arches. I needed that distraction and for him it was the equivalent of taking me to a four-star Michelin restaurant.

I know this is a lot of small detail, but I believe everything I tell you is connected or is the consequence of a larger design. At this stage, I have had the terrible night at Sian's, the disappearance of Lennie, and illness and depression like I have never felt before. It was like something had been set in motion, and that it was gathering momentum with every passing day.

Adrian drove me to Pembroke Dock and we crossed the long toll bridge. I looked out across the estuary. I remember how the sun was beginning to set. It was early still, maybe six. The refinery and oil tankers had their own kind of beauty with all the lights. One of the stacks had a huge flame spurting from it and it always reminded me of one of my favourite movies, *Blade Runner*. I remember that night so clearly. I close my eyes and I can see all the little boats bobbing quietly on the water. The sun was reflecting off the windows of the houses on the waterside. The sky was painted with pinks and reds. It was warm in the car and Adrian was playing some Arcade Fire. One positive thing about Adrian was that he did have great taste in music.

We decided to use the drive-through and then eat a little way off. Past the supermarket is a little car park, like a concrete harbour, called Hobbs Point. We were the only car there. Across the estuary was Neyland town. All the lights were on in the windows as people had gotten home, and were sat down to eat and watch TV. I do miss that. I want you to understand that. I miss someone asking me how my day was. Or getting home and talking to someone or looking forward to sharing dinner. These are things we take for granted. I need you to understand that I am not some crazy cat woman. I don't even have a cat. That is how afraid I am. I am afraid that a defenceless animal will be hurt just by being around me. I don't want to be alone. I don't want to be on my own anymore. I just want a normal life again.

We sat there. Adrian was a noisy eater. It annoyed me. I believe it is called misophonia; it's a mental condition where certain sounds can really irritate you. That is what I read. We were sat there looking across the water. It was dark by then and I still felt ill and tired, and I was not enjoying the food. If anything it was making me feel worse, but I was glad to be out.

On the water, there were loads of lights. There were lights of boats, lights from the buoys and reflections of light from the refinery and oil tankers. I noticed one bright orange light. It was higher than the boats on the estuary. It just hung there. It was swaying ever so gently. I thought it must be a light on a mast of a boat hidden out in the darkness. The light seemed to get bigger. I pointed it out to Adrian who said it was the light of a tug. I wanted to believe him, but it just didn't settle with me. I had a sick feeling in my stomach, and I felt the electricity in the air, literally in the car. The windows were definitely closed as it was a cold night.

The light grew bigger and I realised it was moving at quite some speed. I convinced myself it had to be a large boat or possibly an aircraft. The light got closer, a bright orange ball. It seemed almost to be a flame, like it was a ball of fire trapped in a glass ball. Adrian looked distraught. He said whatever it was, it was going to hit the car park. He tried to start the car, but the engine wouldn't take. I instinctively threw up my arms in front of my face but the ball was upon us, and suddenly came to a standstill and hovered above us for a few seconds. We were bathed in its orange fiery glow. Everything in the car was dead and the air was charged with static. I could hear the popping as a result of air rapidly expanding and collapsing in the car. The ball must have hovered silently there for a few seconds and then it shot off at great speed down the estuary towards the bridge. The static charge in the car dissipated. It was all over in a few seconds. Maybe it was four, maybe five seconds in total.

Adrian was understandably flustered. He chattered excitedly about UFOs and top-secret military aircraft. He was annoyed that he did not react quick enough to take a picture, but I silently knew that our phones would not have worked. I felt the same dread and panic I had had at the farmhouse. Adrian said that we had been *buzzed* and that we had just seen a UFO.

There could be no way that the two events were related. There was no conceivable way that something was following me and was brash enough to do it on a busy waterway early on a weekday evening, but, Mr Davies, you do know don't you? You do know there were reports that evening, don't you? People all along the estuary spotted a bright orange ball hovering and then travelling at high speed over the water. There were reports that the object darted amongst the ships and eventually was seen making its way back out towards the sea.*

There were reports on the date given of unusual activity on the estuary that night. Several anglers saw the object as well as motorists crossing the Cleddau Bridge. The object as described on the estuary is not uncommon with other sightings again on the 22nd March 2009 and 4th April 2009. The alleged object exhibited the same behavioural patterns applied as to the sighting made by Susan. Over twenty witnesses at Hobbs Point claim they saw an orange ball navigating the estuary and its flight was monitored by a tug. The tug was said to have used its searchlight to track the object for a time before it took off at great velocity. No one could dismiss it as a "normal" sighting or occurrence. Again, a similar sighting was reported in 2004 of a large fiery ball moving at speed and varying heights on the Cleddau Estuary. There is no explanation currently to the origin of the object though one source claims that he had witnessed a stealth class destroyer navigating its way up the estuary one night in early 2010 which may or may not be related to these incidents.

I saw it up close and personal. I felt the energy pulsating off that object as it hung there, curious. I feel like it scanned us. I cannot prove that it did such a thing, but I felt like it was examining us. I cannot say that it came purposefully to investigate me, but it was too close of a coincidence that within three days I had been involved in a strange occurrence with strange lights and dreams of alien-like creatures. I was beyond terrified if I am perfectly honest. I felt helpless. Adrian got the car started and drove at speed to get over the bridge and to park by the pub on the waterside at Burton.

As we drove, Adrian chattered excitedly between mouthfuls of his burger. He thought it was a UFO but said that the military had new craft that we were not aware of. Perhaps it was an unmanned drone, a probe of some description. We drove towards a pub on the side of the estuary on the other side of the bridge.

He was soon on his phone ringing his friends. He was trying to get a search party together, a posse to stake out the estuary to see if the object came back.

I have had over five years to think through what I saw that night but my immediate reaction was not so much, "What was it?" but, "Who was it?" I was shaken up, as it seemed so close to the events of the weekend. I was starting to doubt that the events were ordinary at all, but really? Why would an unknown craft have an interest in an ordinary woman? I am nothing special – why pick me out?

I did not believe it was man-made. Its design was nothing like that of an aircraft. Perhaps it was a weather phenomenon? It must be explainable. But there had been the weekend, and now this. I felt frightened. I selfishly hoped that this was happening all over the world. I wanted to imagine reporters and experts trying to make sense of a global epidemic of sightings across the planet. That way I knew it would not be just me. I even hoped it was an invasion. It sounds ridiculous now, but these were my immediate thoughts.

When we parked at the waterside pub, I turned on the radio. I tuned to the local station, hoping there would be chatter about the sighting but there was just a song playing. Adrian turned off the radio and snapped at me saying impatiently that he was on the phone. I sat there staring into the night just wanting to leave, to get as far away as possible, and not be so close to the water's edge. I imagined the water swelling up and rising with waves crashing around the car, and the glowing ball emerging from the dark oily water and consuming us in its fire.

Adrian got off the phone and I asked him if he would take me home. He got very angry with me saying I was selfish, and that something amazing was going on and he wanted to see if it came back. He said this could be something that changed the world, changed everything and he told me he would see if there was a bus going back to Haverfordwest for me. He dropped me at the bus stop in Pembroke Dock and didn't even wait with me. He sped off and I waited there mortified and frankly terrified that the ball of light might come back for me, to carry me off or burn me.

The bus arrived, and I sat on it and cried. I cried because in my reflection in the window I saw a trickle of blood flow from my nose. I was sick and run-down, frightened and lonely. I felt so depressed, a well of anxiety deep in my stomach. I had no idea what was going on, I just wanted this to be an awful horrid nightmare that I would snap out of and be back in the apartment with Lennie snoozing on the bed or licking my face wanting to be let out to go for a pee.

There was another man on the bus sat near the back and I felt an unnatural distrust for him. He did absolutely nothing to warrant such feeling, but I just felt like he was staring at me the whole time. I imagined wherever I was, I was being watched. I was so paranoid and it's a feeling that has rarely left me ever since. Your interview technique is very effective, Mr Davies, you are certainly bringing me back into these moments. I feel as sick and as frightened as I did then.

I got back home around eight. I was still living with my aunt at this time in the centre of Pembrokeshire. My parents lived far away in the northeast of the county and it was convenient for me to live with her. It was easy to drive to the university and if something happened to my car then I could commute by train or bus. I had part-time work in Haverfordwest too, nothing taxing or beneficial to my studies but it was money, plus my aunty had experienced a nasty break-up and she enjoyed having my company. We didn't see each other that often as she worked nights but when we did it was good fun and good company.

My aunt was not at home, but her cat was. Mog, not the most imaginative name for a cat I will admit, was a beautiful black cat. She was still young, and her mewing and rubbing against my legs was as welcome as a deep hug when I stepped into the house. I was tempted to ring my mother and tell her everything, but what would I say? That I had seen strange figures in a dream and a UFO while eating a burger with that absolute bell-end Adrian? It sounded stupid; you don't discuss those kind of things with my mother. I thought I would sleep on it and see how I felt in the morning.

I checked the news, checked websites and social media, and there was nothing about the object. I felt hurt by Adrian but, in hindsight, who could blame him? It was like nothing either of us had seen before. I just wished he had been mature enough to think of how I felt being left alone like that. I think if I had not had the experience of that weekend that I would have happily joined him on his stakeout, but it was all too closely linked and connected for my liking.

It was over for Adrian and I after that night. He tried to text me on the weekend, late one night. He had been wanting sex, but I ignored him, and a week later he and a new girl were plastered all over his Facebook page. "It is what it is," as so many are so fond of saying. I am not angry with him; in a way I am glad as I genuinely did not want to get anyone involved in all this and get them hurt. That was the last time I had any form of romantic relationship, if you could call it that between us.

I showered. I needed to, I had terrible diarrhoea and was clammy from sweating. I felt atrocious. I did feel safe in the familiar surroundings, knowing that Aunty would be back in the morning. Her house was in a built-up area, surrounded by houses, cars coming and going, people walking by, dog walkers, reassuringly far from the isolation of Sian's farmhouse. I went to bed and lay there. But every time I closed my eyes I could see the great fiery globe silently hovering above the black water, as if it was looking for me, calling out my name. I know I keep repeating that, but it really did feel that way.

I turned on the TV in my bedroom and had the volume on low. I just wanted the light and company. It made me feel safer. I eventually dropped off. That night I had the first of three terrible nights. Three nights that defied anything I could even begin to understand.

Holocaust

"For behold, the day is coming, burning like a furnace; and all the arrogant and every evildoer will be chaff; and the day that is coming will set them ablaze," says the LORD of hosts, "so that it will leave them neither root nor branch."
Malachi 4:1

Susan: I'm not insane. I'm sure I'm not. I didn't go looking for these kinds of experiences. The odd daydream, OK, but I didn't use to fantasize. I just wanted to get on with a normal life. Now, I sit here with you as the sun begins to set knowing in a few hours I will have to try and fight sleep again, and that feeling of dread chills me at the end of every single day. I've studied sleep disorders, sleep paralysis and the like, trying to make sense of what's been happening, but it's all too vivid to be just a dream. I survive on very little sleep now. Sleep has become my enemy, it makes me vulnerable, but I guess that if these things are coming for me it doesn't matter whether I'm conscious or not. You will understand more after I explain what happened.

That first night, I fell into a deep sleep.

I found myself walking a dark country lane. I could hear the wind in the trees and I was walking with a tall man. I can't see his face, but he is holding my hand in his. I feel very small; his hand seems gigantic compared to mine. I think I must be a little girl, but I can't recall this event ever happening in my life. I don't think this is a memory. I try to peek at the man's face, but it's in shadow. I feel the chill of the night on my face and on my knees, which makes me think I am wearing a skirt or dress. The sky is cloudy and there is no moon or starlight. I don't know where we are going but I do not feel afraid; I feel safe and calm with my faceless walking companion.

Suddenly there is a bright light from behind us and the road is illuminated. Our shadows are stretched up the road. I hear a man's voice say, *"We have to run now, don't look behind."* I think, "Why do we have to run? It's just a car driving from behind, and if we stop and stay to the side of the road the car will pass and we will be fine." But the light becomes intense and we run. The man takes great strides and I struggle to keep up. There is a blinding flash and I scream as I feel the man's hand let go of mine.

I find myself halfway along the High Street in Haverfordwest. I am walking down the hill flanked by the big old buildings on either side. It is snowing. There are Christmas lights everywhere. They are draped high across the streets, in shop windows and on the roofs of the buildings in the town centre. In this part of the dream Castle Square at the bottom of the High Street has a huge fir tree covered in Christmas lights. The snow is quite deep as I trudge through it, and I clearly think to myself that it must be late as there are no other footprints in the snow, not even tyre tracks. It is wonderful and beautiful, just like a scene from a movie. I feel as if this has been done for me; it's my own private moment, a truly beautiful moment. I get the sense that I am meeting someone, maybe some friends. Maybe I am on a night out. I feel the chill in the air, but I do not feel uncomfortable. It is magical.

At the bottom of the High Street the pubs there are closed but I look right towards Quay Street and again see Christmas lights, and also a bright, warm glow. It's the doorway of a bar that is not usually there. I walk into the light and climb up some stairs. It is warm and cosy in contrast to the chill outside. *Lonely This Christmas*, that song by Mud, is playing on a jukebox. The bar has Christmas lights draped above it. There are half a dozen small round tables in the room, all empty, and padded high-backed benches along each wall. I am alone in here, but I don't feel uncomfortable or feel that I am trespassing. I call out, but no words come from my voice. I turn toward the bar and placed there is a glass of mulled wine. There is steam floating off the top as if it has been freshly heated and poured. I take a sip and feel the warmth fill my chest and belly. I feel all the tenseness in my shoulders drift away and I feel relaxed and content, a real good Christmas feeling. I notice in the mirror behind the bar a figure walking past and it sits at one of the small round tables.

I spin around and sat there is a woman. I recognize her. It's my grandmother. I drop the glass and it smashes silently on the floor. My gran had died of cancer when I was ten. I was shocked to see her, but I didn't feel afraid. My gran was a wonderful, kind woman, so energetic, so full of life. She lived every day as if it were her last and here she sat, as if I had never lost her.

I walked over, and I heard her voice. Her mouth never opened but I heard her voice clearly in my mind. She said I looked well and she was very proud of how hard I was working and for looking after my aunty. She asked me to sit down and I did almost involuntarily. I just gazed at her, she looked so well. I wanted to ask her how she was and as I thought this she replied *dandy*. Gran always used to say dandy whenever she was asked how she was. I remember as a little girl going to see her in the hospital for what turned out to be the last time. She lay in a bed, tubes sticking from her, an oxygen mask covering her face. She looked so ill, so thin and her skin looked like paper. The vibrancy had gone. All that was left was a body being consumed from within. I was a little afraid to see her like that, but my mother said to talk to her, so I asked her how she was, and in a weak and raspy voice she replied *dandy*. I loved her so much.

Yet here she was so healthy, so alive. Gran looked at me with her wonderful green eyes and I heard her voice again. She said that I had to help some of her friends. They needed my help and I had to be brave, and no matter what happened she was here with me. She reached across the table and held my hand. Her hand was warm and reassuring. Her voice then said that they were here. The jukebox stopped and the lights in the bar dimmed until it felt as if there was just a spotlight shining down upon us. I sensed several people in the shadows. From the corner of my eye I could make out a blurry shadowy figure.

There was a tremendous pain in my head and a flash before my eyes. I felt as if something was sticking into the back of my head. I was unable to move, I was unable to scream. I could not see Gran or feel her hand hold mine anymore. The pain in my head was excruciating and I literally thought my head was going to implode. It was as if something was being sucked out. I lost all vision and was plunged into darkness. I could hear a scream. I think it was my own.

I found myself in a cinema. In front of me were rows and rows of plush red seats and a huge cinema screen. It looked like the one in Haverfordwest that I used to go to with my parents. I could not move but I was aware that there was someone sat behind me. Above I could see the projector light beam across the darkness and illuminate the screen. It felt so real that I could even smell the popcorn.

I sat there confused, wondering where my gran had gone when the screen started into life. It was a film about here, about Pembrokeshire. There was no music, no narration, no sound at all. I saw Haverfordwest from the air on a beautiful summer's day, the castle and the river, the houses and the trees. I saw Milford Haven from the waterway and then the Preseli Hills and fields and woodlands. The film showed a point of view shot of a roller coaster at the local theme park and then a water slide. All the beautiful beaches flashed before me. I saw the Narberth Winter Carnival with all its floats covered in lights and then hundreds of people dashing into the grey waves at Tenby for the Boxing Day swim. I saw mothers sat in a circle at a crèche clapping in unison with their little toddlers. I saw the huge oil tankers parked up on the Milford Haven waterway, and people leaving a supermarket and filling their car up with shopping and then driving off.

Then the film became more surreal, more disturbing. I was shown a close-up of hundreds of ants trying to pull a fat-bellied spider into a small hole. The hole in the earth was too small for the spider to fit but the ants pulled at its legs, desperate to get it into the hole. It was a garden spider, brown with a white cross on its back. It would try and escape, but the ants were swarming, overwhelming it. Some of them pulled off a leg and disappeared with it down the hole like it was a prized tree branch. The spider gave a last desperate surge of energy to try and get away, but it was useless.

The ants swarmed over the spider's head pulling at its eyes, and formed a chain around its fat body, pulling at it. I felt uneasy, ill, and wanted the film to end. But I could not look away or even close my eyes. It was like that scene in *A Clockwork Orange*. The spider's head tore from its body and ants disappeared with it down the hole. The sea of ants became more excited and the spider's body began to swell and contract. It tore apart, a great big gash opened, and hundreds of tiny spiders emerged. The ants carried the tiny spiders into the hole. It was horrific to watch. It just didn't make sense.

There was another sharp pain in my head, a flash of light and then blackness.

I heard my grandmother's voice faintly say *dandy*.

I woke up in my bed. The TV was still on. It was still night time. I sat up. The pain in my head was awful and my mouth was so dry. I was so thirsty. It had been an awful nightmare, one that I thought I would never wake up from. I saw a light on the landing from under the door and heard a noise. I hoped my aunty was back. I needed to talk to her, to someone. I got out of bed. My legs were so weak, that it took me a while to stand. I had awful pains in my stomach, sharp stabbing pains, and desperately needed the toilet. I opened my bedroom door and there before me was a skinny, faceless, black figure.

It touched me on the side of the head with a black metal claw-like hand and I screamed.

I woke up again and I was back in my bed. Light was pouring in through the gaps in the curtains. The TV was still on and I looked at my clock and it was gone eleven. I had slept 13 hours, yet I felt exhausted. I was so dismayed by the nightmares. Normally the memory of dreams becomes more fragmented as the day passes. But I remembered everything of this, all the detail, the pains, the lights, the images, the film, my gran, the skinny faceless shadow man at my bedroom door. I remember it five years later as if it had just happened.

I started thinking about what all of this meant. I looked back at the weekend at Sian's, the light Adrian and I had seen on the estuary. I had a feeling that last night was not just a nightmare but something I had actually experienced, yet none of it made any sense. I was terrified beyond belief.

I sat on my bed emotional and mentally drained, and began to cry. I could not fathom what was happening or how this was happening. I questioned if any of this was real. I always believed I was a rational person. Maybe I'd had a breakdown and I would wake in a bed in a hospital or in a mental health institution. I wondered if I'd been in an accident and was in a coma. Maybe I had not made it to Sian's that night and was in an ambulance after a nasty crash being pumped full of drugs. I had all these maybes and possible explanations, but nothing had changed inside. I was still sat on the bed in my room with all the recent experiences fresh in my mind. If this was not real, I could not find a way to snap out of it.

I looked at my bed and was appalled and ashamed that I had wet myself. A yellow stain spread across the bed sheets, my pyjama bottoms smelling of piss.

I rushed out of my room and I was sick in the toilet. All that week I hardly kept any food down. I heard a voice call up from downstairs. It was my aunty. I was so relieved to hear her. I made my way downstairs and she was sat watching TV in the living room. I have never been so comforted in all my life to see another human being. She took one look at me and stood up and asked if I was OK. She looked appalled. I must have looked terrible. I hugged her and I began to sob uncontrollably. My aunty was shocked; she had never seen me like this. She fired questions at me. Had someone hurt me? Had Adrian and I had a row?

She sat me down and I babbled to her about everything from Sian's to my dream last night. She looked at me, she was speechless. I guess, how would you respond to all that? She asked if I had taken any drugs, had I been spiked, and I reassured her that I had not. She thought that maybe the strains of the coursework and study had taken its toll on me. She said I was driven and relentless in my pursuit to achieve and that maybe I just needed a holiday. I asked her about the fiery globe on the water and she said that maybe it was real, maybe it was a military experiment, or something created by all the gases and pollution of the refineries. She said that it was possible; she had seen a documentary on such phenomena and coupled with a few bad dreams and coincidences it had made everything seem so much more real to me.

I had doubts, but I was happy to accept her logic. She began to play detective and thought that maybe Lennie the dog had found a way out of the apartment and into the garage beneath and escaped. Or maybe one of the girls had taken him out early in the morning and lost him. Perhaps they were too ashamed to admit it, and let me take the blame for it. She said that a million things could have caused all of this.

Aunty made me a cup of tea and some toast. She said she would run a bath for me, and call the university and say I would not be in for the rest of the week. She had said she was off that night and she, Mog and I would watch some TV and films, and have a good old rest and catch up. She promised me that by the next day I would be feeling much better.

I did feel a bit better for having the company, and I felt safe lying there on the settee. My mind wandered back to the dream. Aunty had said sleep paralysis could be caused by stress and exhaustion, and perhaps that was behind it all. But I felt sad having seen Gran so vividly, and disturbed at seeing the spider so cruelly killed by the ants. It made no sense at that time.

The evening came, and Aunty and I had supper and she handed me two sleeping tablets. She said to take them, and I would be out like a light in next to no time. She said she would keep her bedroom door open, so she could keep an eye on me. Our rooms were opposite each other so we would be able to see each other. It made a huge difference to how I felt. Having that company, that security, made me feel the most relaxed I had felt all that week.

I got into bed and I looked across from my door and saw Aunty sat in her bed reading. Mogs was asleep, lying next to her. It made me feel so happy seeing them both. I do remember the tablets working. My eyes were heavy, and my body felt like lead. Inside I remember feeling a contentedness. I quickly fell asleep.

I was back on the road again with the strange man in the darkness.

The same thing was happening again, exactly as it had the night before. The car light, I assumed it was a car, came from behind and we started to run. The man let go and I screamed.

Then I was back on the snow-covered High Street in Haverfordwest. The scene was exactly as it had been the night before. I had the same feelings. The feeling of this being my own private moment. The light was shining in the street, inviting, and I made my way towards it. I was reliving the dream from the night before. I looked behind me as I entered the doorway and there was no sign of life. I think I expected to see shadowy figures start to emerge from the doorways and creep towards me. I expected a trap.

Inside the bar the Christmas music played on the jukebox and a glass of warm mulled wine was waiting for me on the bar.

I was nervous this time and on edge as I looked around for the shadowy people that I knew would attack me. I waited for Gran. She did not appear.

I turned my back on the room and looked into the mirror behind the bar and again, like last time, I saw a figure walk past and sit down at the centre table. I spun around as I was desperate to talk to Gran to find out what was happening; why she had left me and why had she let them hurt me.

Instead of Gran sat there, I saw a little girl. She was about seven years old, with her blonde hair tied into two pigtails. She wore a familiar red dress and little black shoes. I dropped my glass; again, it smashed silently on the floor. I knew this little girl. This little girl was me. This was me from all those years ago. She said to sit. I did so. I was trembling. I was so frightened and confused. I heard her; I heard my own young voice in my own head. The voice said not to panic, that what had happened last night was not going to happen again tonight. The voice said that I had done well, and her friends had been very grateful for my help and sorry if it had upset me.

I just stared at my younger self. She smiled. It's hard to explain, you can go mad trying to make sense of this. The little girl said that she was going to ask some questions and then I could go home. She said I did not have to speak but just answer in my mind. She said that her friends could read thoughts, and the pictures my mind made would be my answer.

I was unable to answer back but I said OK in my mind. The little girl flashed a big smile, with a tooth missing, one I remember losing as a child.

She asked me if I had a baby would I love it more than my own life. I was confused and found it difficult to relate to at first, and I heard a new voice, deep and empty and sexless say, *"She won't."* This was not my voice or the voice of the younger me but of someone unseen. As I was thinking of my answers it was as if someone was relaying my answers to someone else. I shouted in my mind that I would, that I would love my child's life more than my own.

I was then asked if I would kill a man to protect myself. I tried to shut my mind down, to keep it blank but I thought of killing someone if I was being attacked. I thought about defending myself, of lashing out, to survive at all costs and I heard the voice again say, *"Killer."*

The younger version of me asked if I had to choose between my father and my mother to save from a fire then who I would save. I thought of my dad running to pick me up when I was a child. It was a flashback, from when I was stung by a bee and how safe I felt with him, and I thought of a row Mother and I had the day I left home. I tried to blank out my thoughts, but it was an immediate initial response. I felt like I was betraying myself. The deep voice affirmed, *"Father."* I screamed in my mind that I would save them both, that this was stupid and meant nothing. I was overwhelmed by guilt. I love both my mother and my father. You must understand this. They must know this. When I am gone, they must know I loved them both.

The younger version of me asked if I was raped would I enjoy the experience. My mind screamed, *"NO!"* I envisioned an awful, ugly man attacking me and brutalizing me, treating me like a lump of meat, indifferent to my rights as a person, stabbing and violating, unloving and brutal. The voice deep and strange said, *"Yes."* I shouted in my mind, what kind of stupid answer was that? I was furious, and I hurled obscenities at the unknown person behind the voice. I called it a cowardly sick mother fucker. I looked at the innocence of my young face before me and I was so angry that I could be subjected to this in such a demeaning way. There was no way at that age I would have talked about such inappropriate things. I was asked many more questions. Some were dull, some were infuriating, some deeply personal and others truly pointless. I felt exhausted. I just wanted to wake up and be done with it.

Finally, the little girl, my younger self, stood up and she said thank you, and I had been very helpful and that her friends were satisfied with my efforts. She said there would be a quick moment of unpleasantness and then it would be all over. Before I had time to panic there was a sharp pain in my head and a blinding flash. It was agonizing. It was as if my mind was imploding.

I woke up in bed. I was unable to move. I felt a huge pressure on my chest, just like the sleep paralysis that Aunty had spoken about. There was a rushing in my ears and a weight on my chest. I shifted my eyes to my right and I could see Aunty and Mogs across the hall asleep in their bed. Aunty had left her light on. I saw a tall slim hazy figure pass in the hallway. Then I saw something that was so unbelievably strange in my aunt's bedroom. I can only describe it as like a jellyfish. On top of her bed was this thing. It had a large bulbous transparent mass for a body that was filled with what looked like bio-illuminated lights, like the sort of lights you see on creatures deep under the sea. The jelly-like mass was supported by incredibly thin segmented legs, like the legs of an insect, but so thin, it seemed that it would be impossible to support the body on top. The lights in the body flashed reds, yellows and blues. There seemed to be a sack on its back, like a lung that was opening and closing and emitting a yellow mist or gas. It was on top of my aunt. I tried to scream, I wanted to wake her up and warn her. I wanted to get up, throw the nearest thing at it, to run in there and tear that creature from her bed. I wanted to stomp on it until it was no more than a slimy pulp.

The creature got close to my aunty's face and two long thin vein-like tendrils emerged from the area where a head would be. One tendril moved up to my aunt's face and it entered her nose while the other stretched and moved on to the face of Mogs. My aunty lay there while this thing stood above her, its tendril stretching, unwinding, into her nostril. I imagined it deep within her stomach, feeling around, planting eggs or seeds or sucking the life from her.

Then Mogs started to lift into the air. This must sound surreal. She was still asleep, and she was a few feet off the bed, held up by the tendril that I could see had entered her mouth. Her little furry body hung limp. The Creature began to quiver and the colours in its mass changed colours more rapidly. I saw my aunty wake up and she screamed.

I woke up. I was lying in my bed and the daylight was streaming through the gaps in the curtain. My mouth was dry, and my head was pounding. There was the sharp pain behind my eye which would become common after such events. I sat up and looked around my room. The door was still open, and I could see into my aunt's bedroom. She was not in her bed and her duvet was a crumpled heap on her bedroom floor.

I could hear retching and heaving, the all too familiar sound of vomit splashing and echoing in a toilet bowl. I hopped up out of bed and the room swam. I felt so disorientated and hugged the wall to get into the hallway and to the bathroom. My aunty was hunched over the toilet bowl and was being sick. I felt nauseous just smelling the bathroom. I asked if she was OK, and she gave me a thumbs up and continued retching. I rubbed her back and went to the sink to get her a glass of water. The porcelain was splattered with blood; it was like a sky of red stars on a white background. I washed out the sink and got her some water.

She just sat there hugging the bowl. I did not know what to say to her. The last time I had seen her she had been violated by some strange jellyfish creature. I thought that must be a dream, right? I was too frightened to blurt out what I had seen. Was it just a dream? I asked her what she thought might have caused this sickness and she replied that there was a bug going around at work. I remember her words echoing in the bowl and how alien it made her sound. She motioned for me to leave her as she did not want me to get ill.

She sat up and her hair was matted to her face, and there was blood around her nose and top lip. I asked what had happened to her face and she laughed and said God had made her that way and she had to live with what she was given. She was a striking woman, very beautiful and still only in her late forties. I asked her about the blood and she said she must have retched so hard that it must have caused a nosebleed.

I finally helped her up and put her back to bed. I picked up the duvet and tucked her in. I opened her window to let some fresh air in as it was stinking in there, and went downstairs and made her a cuppa. Mogs was lying on her armchair in the living room and looked awful. Her eyes were all puffy and her nose looked raw as if she had been rubbing it. I started to panic. I started to think that something had happened to both of them in the night. It was not a coincidence, it was not a dream. It could not be.

I put food on a saucer for Mogs and brought a fresh glass of water up for my aunt. My aunt just lay there, and I offered to call a doctor, and she said some sleep and the water was fine. She said she was exhausted and just needed to rest.

I spent the morning online reading to see if anyone else had these weird dreams and visions. There were hundreds of links to alien visitation, to demons and dimensional beings, to ghosts and paranormal creatures. I was at this time still thinking I was having some kind of psychological breakdown. I researched the strange orange globe on the water and saw image after image of UFOs and strange light anomalies. I read people's accounts of alien abduction and experimentation, and all of it made me sick.

The more I read the more I didn't want to be like these people. It seemed to me they were just looking for attention. I called the doctors and made an appointment. They could see me that very day which I was grateful for.

I only told the doctor that I was not sleeping, and was having strange sensations and seeing things I did not think could be there. I was told I had an iron deficiency and that it sounded like I had elevated adrenaline levels which were causing anxiety, which in turn was causing sleep disorders and panic attacks. The doctor said it was not uncommon for sleep paralysis to be a symptom. I told her about the demon-like creatures, ghosts and aliens I'd seen. She laughed, and said there was nothing to worry about, they were not real. She prescribed tablets to help with my anxiety levels and sleeping tablets to help me rest. She also gave me advice on my diet and lifestyle. I really wanted her to be right. If the tablets stopped this madness and allowed me to continue with my life then I would have been truly grateful.

I got home, and Aunty was lying on the settee. She said she felt better even though she did not look it and was excited to see what drugs I had brought home. I refused to give her the anti-anxiety pills which made her throw a cushion at me. She said she was concerned by Mogs as she had not eaten all day and had pooped on the armchair where she lay. The cat had been too ill to get up and use the cat litter tray. I said I would take her the vets in the morning if she was not better, but Aunty said she would do it. Mogs looked awful. Her eyes were practically swollen shut. Aunty had cleaned her up and put her on some newspaper and put a bowl of food and water on the fireplace by the armchair. The three of us made a pitiful sight. I will admit despite everything that I was excited to go to bed that night. I had to be brave and believe that this was nothing but bad brain chemicals and hormones, and that some pills and a good night's sleep at last would solve this. In hindsight, maybe I should not have been so optimistic especially with how Aunty and Mogs were, but I needed some hope to hold on to. After the weekend I would be better, I would go back to college and get back to studying and working hard and look to make amends with Sian. I felt positive for the first time all week.

That night I made sure Aunty had everything she needed, and I took my tablets and went up to bed. Aunty decided she was going to stay on the settee and watch some movies. I lay in bed in the darkness and I shut down my mind from the negativity, the sickness and all the worrying things that had happened in the week. I focused on only the good things in life. I thought about the summer and good friends and family. I imagined dancing to my favourite songs and of lazy sunny days sat on the beach with my head stuck in a good book. As I thought of all these wonderful things I drifted off into sleep.

I was back.

It was like *Groundhog Day*. I was back on the dark road with the man, the light bright behind us and then back in the town with the snow and Christmas lights. This time I did not want to go to the glowing light on the street. I wanted to run away, find someone, find somewhere where I could be safe and not have to answer questions or witness creatures being killed. As much as I did not want to enter the bar I found myself drawn to it, like a moth to a flame. The bar was set up exactly as it had been the previous two nights. The same song was playing on the jukebox.

In each dream I tried to resist the urge to follow the set path, but it was useless, and I found myself interacting with the setting the same way I always did. I thought I had a choice of actions but in fact I had none; it was like I was being led. I reached out and drank the mulled wine and stared into the mirror behind the bar, and behind me a shadow figure appeared and sat at the centre table. I dreaded to think who it might be this time, and as I turned it was not a younger version of myself or my gran but Sian, my friend. I was so glad to see her. I had not seen her in a few days and I missed her terribly. I just needed to talk to her, to make amends.

This time, though, I did not drop the glass and I made my way over to the table to talk to her. Again, like before I could hear her voice in my mind, but her mouth never opened. She just sat there and smiled. She said in my mind that this was going to the last meeting like this and that no matter what would happen that I would have to remember that this would be it.

She said that it was not my fault about Lennie and that her friends had him. She said all I had to do was concentrate and it would soon be over. She said that I had to be brave. But the more her face stared at me, smiling, the more I began to panic. Sian looked up from my face and over my shoulder and I heard her voice say they were here. The jukebox stopped, and the lights went dim.

They were back; I could sense them all around me in the shadows.

Watching.

I pleaded in my mind for Sian to help me, to help me escape; to get me back into the snow-covered streets. I was terrified. I would imagine it would be like someone waking up and discovering they were paralysed. Utter helplessness. I felt someone close. There was a flash and a terrible pain.

I was sat back in the cinema as I had been the first night. The projector light flickered above me and I had the sense that despite the cinema seeming empty that there were people sat behind me. I believe it was the same people responsible for all of this. Again, I could not move and only look forward. I could not even blink. The screen came on and a film began to play.

It was Pembrokeshire again. I was shown the county from above and then from street level. I saw luscious woodlands and fields, clear streams flowing in the hills and people cycling through fallen red leaves on an autumn day. There was no sound, no music or narration just the blissful views of Pembrokeshire. There were children playing at the school where I used to go, and boats sailing on the estuary by the pub Adrian and I had sat that night. The water and sky were blue, and the sun shone brightly. I saw old people sat at Broad Haven beach enjoying an ice cream and a marching band walk through Haverfordwest on a bright summer's day as people lined the street. I saw mothers and dads cheering their children on during a sports day and the ferry sailing up the blue water passing unloading super oil tankers on the Milford Haven estuary.

Then it changed.

There was a rumble, I could hear water sloshing, birds screeching high above.

This time the film lingered on the ferry sailing up the estuary, the same estuary I had seen the orange object on. The sky had been blue, and it suddenly went very dark. I could see the water become choppier and then the choppiness become big waves. The sky was now black, like night, even though it had just been daytime, and the refinery glowed an intense orange. I think it was on fire.

It seemed the estuary took a deep breath, sucking up the water, moving it back up towards the bridge, the ferry, and the boats and the oil tankers were all swaying and bobbing. I could even taste the air, a smell of burning, like chemicals and burning rubber, a suffocating stench.

I needed to warn someone that something terrible was happening but then there was a huge explosion of light that filled the screen and then the sea came rushing down through the estuary, but this time it was on fire. The ferry and the tankers were tossed and turned by a huge wave of fire and debris. It was like a fiery version of the Japanese tsunami that had been shown so much on the news at the time. The waves must have been twenty feet high. People ran past on the street next to the surging water, screaming and panicking. I can see it was the front street of Milford Haven. The wave was an unstoppable wall of dirty water and fire. I prayed people were running to higher ground, getting to safety.

A car flew past, literally tumbling through the air, and you could see the driver inside, an elderly woman, screaming as her car smashed into other cars on the road. A fat man in a suit was melting like wax; he was emitting a sound more like that of an animal than a human. One woman fell as she carried a child, her hand held against the child's head to protect it, but she could not run fast enough, and the fiery water engulfed them both and swept them away in a flow of flame and debris. Houses were toppling over into the torrent of destruction like mud. There was a smaller explosion, and parts of people, limbs, heads scattered across the screen.

An oil tanker rolled and floated upside down engulfed in the flames and exploded, shaking the camera and levelling what was left of the street. The sky was black with smoke and the water was just a sea of orange intense fire. The ferry was still moving, and I could see people on the deck running; there were people on fire. I could hear what sounded like a thousand different screams. I did not want to see any more of this. I was terrified; I was witnessing a disaster that was destroying a whole town, maybe it was the end of the world. I had seen people die in the most awful ways, and I had seen destruction and chaos like hell on earth, and there was nothing I could do to save anyone. I have never felt so useless in my whole life.

The screen finally faded to black.

I was so relieved that the horror was over. I knew that next I would feel the pain in my head, but I hoped that Sian had not lied when she said that this would be the last time; this would be the final encounter. The image of the ants and the spiders was nothing compared to what I had just seen. I waited for the pain and the flash but instead the screen came back to life.

The film showed a dark sky lit by the glow of so many fires. It showed a crater of rubble and fire of where the town of Milford had been. The remains of the ferry lay, belly up, in the crater like a carcass. The camera left the scene and showed me a little child, a toddler sat on some rubble crying, its clothes scorched and tattered. I wanted to reach out and grab it, to hold it. Its face was so black from the smoke and its hair so singed that I could not tell if it was a boy or a girl.

The scene changed, and two old people hung on to each other.

They seemed to be stuck under what looked like the remains of a burnt and crushed car. The woman's head that the man was holding on to had been crushed. Her blood and brains were all over his face. The old man sobbed with grief. I did not want to watch this. It was so real, so vivid, I wanted to reach out and help. This was more than a Hollywood movie. I was witnessing the aftermath of a horrific and devastating disaster. I was there but powerless to help.

The cinema screen showed a school playground. Dozens of children lay on the ground as black soot fell from the blackened sky like snow. The school behind them was a pile of rubble. I was shown Haverfordwest where the marching band and the spectators were strewn lifeless, smashed and broken across the street like dolls. The band's musical instruments were twisted and broken amongst the bricks and wreckage on the road. Many of the buildings had collapsed and some burned brightly against the backdrop of the hellish sky.

I was shown a figure, its hair and clothes gone from the fire, its skin red and raw, crawl across the ground and try and reach the small body of a child. I recognized the place as the location of the school sports day. I was witnessing a woman, despite horrendous injuries and pain, try and help her child. The child was obviously dead, incinerated in the explosion. The skin had gone from its small body and bones were protruding through the flesh. It was horrifying, it was appalling, and I was so disturbed by the hideous and terrible imagery.

I felt my life was pointless. I actually wished I could die, as what hope was there? Something terrible was going to happen and if it didn't then we were all going to die one day regardless and there was nothing we could do to stop it. Everyone you love or care about will die and we will become nothing. I watched the charred woman reach out at the dead child on the scorched playing field. She tugged at the child, pulled at its hand but there was no response, no life from the child that had been so very much alive just moments ago, and the mother gave out a blood-curdling howl. The camera moved up the playing field that now resembled a battleground and zoomed in on her face. It was a mask of red exposed flesh and black soot. I have never seen anything so stomach turning. The woman's blue eyes were filled with tears. Her lips had been burned away exposing broken jagged teeth and a blistered tongue. I wanted to hold her and comfort her as she lived her last agonizing moments. She looked deep into the camera and in an almost inhuman voice said, "*Run.*"

There was a flash of light and the pain in my head returned. I woke up in my room. There were no feelings of sleep paralysis this time. I sat up and looked around the room expecting to see a shadow figure or a weird floating creature. I felt sick and disorientated as if I had been lifted and spun a thousand times in an awful fairground ride. I made it to my feet and pulled open the curtains. I was terrified that I would see a black and charred world. I expected to see a holocaust but instead I was greeted with a fresh winter's morning. I was so thankful that I even thanked God. I think that must have been the last time I ever did that. I cried so much. I sat back down on the bed with my head on my knees sobbing like a child.

What had this dream meant? The imagery of death and destruction was so clear; I felt the pain and anguish of that poor mother. Was I really having a breakdown? I could never conjure up such cruel and horrific images. It's not in my nature to dwell on death and ruin. Was I supposed to warn people or move away to safety? What was it all supposed to mean? Sian in the Christmas bar had said that this would be the last time that this would happen. What had happened to me? Why had my life become so bizarre and so terrifying?

I opened my bedroom door slowly expecting a darky sticklike figure to lunge out at me but there was none. Was this truly over? I was sick as I had been all week and I washed my face.

I looked in the mirror and for a second my face was replaced by the horribly burned face of the mother on the sports field. I began to cry again.

I remembered that Aunty had been poorly and headed downstairs. As I took each step I thought that the dream had told me that this was over; that there would be no more. I needed it to be true; I need to resume my life, yet the image of the disaster flashed in my mind with every blink.

As I got to the bottom of the stairs, I heard a howl. In the living room Aunty was stood there in her pyjamas and I saw that she was crying. She was staring at the armchair. She was staring at Mogs. The cat was dead.

I had hoped this was all over. It was far from over. It will never be over.

Dissemination

The sounds I am listening to every night at first appear to be human voices conversing back and forth in a language I cannot understand. I find it difficult to imagine that I am actually hearing real voices from people not of this planet. There must be a more simple explanation that has so far eluded me.
Nikola Tesla, 1918

It was gone midnight when Susan finished narrating her nightmare. She sat there emotionless, staring at me. The ashtray before her was filled with the stubs of many smoked cigarettes, tombstones of her memories. The day had turned to night and the street below was asleep and bathed in the orange of the street lamp. We both sat there in the silence.

My mind raced at the possibilities. Her account was so three-dimensional, as it were. In a way I enjoyed her rich and descriptive telling, but the feelings of apprehension and dismay were overwhelming.

Could this woman be telling the truth? If this was a hoax, then she had spent a long time conjuring it up, and was a great actress. But were these just nightmares?

It could of course be mental – schizophrenia or schizotypal personality disorder. She could be the victim of very real and vivid delusions. Trapped in a fantasy so intricate that she could no longer separate it from the reality she lived in. Her withdrawal from family and social interaction would tie in with that, and such people could still be highly functioning. But my experience had been that sufferers in this could rarely articulate their delusions so clearly, in such detail. And her life and relationships up to the point of the nightmares had seemed normal.

She finally spoke and asked me if I thought she was lying.

I declined to give a commitment at this time until I could assemble further information. She accepted my response with no emotion, no hint of disappointment or anger. Parts of her record I could examine in further detail, and other parts could only be speculated upon. How do you begin to prove what was just a dream, what was psychosis, and what possibly could be communications from an advanced alien being? And who am I to discern what is real and what is fiction? I'm just reporting what she said, to present as much information as I can to you, the reader.

She took a drag on a freshly-made cigarette that she seemed to magic out of thin air and said that it was rational for me to have doubts; she herself had had plenty of them. We agreed to continue the account the following day. I was eager to record the rest of her testimonial, but I needed to think this over first.

As I descended the dark and unwelcoming steps of her building, I felt a little afraid. There was no way here to conduct a controlled investigation of the kind that I would on an alleged haunting. What could I measure and probe? Regression could prove a useful tool, to see what was in her mind, but she would need to agree to that, and also so many regressive techniques muddy the water rather than clarify it – it wouldn't prove things one way or another. I could encourage her to seek psychiatric evaluation. Though how relevant would that be today for past history? I thought I would definitely encourage her to talk to her doctor again.

I hardly remember the walk home that night, but I do recall staring up at the sky and I imagined seeing an orange ball of fire floating against the stars, hovering there, watching me like the sentinel she had described. I got home mentally exhausted and sat at my desk. I recited Arthur C. Clarke's quote in my mind.

Two possibilities exist: Either we are alone in the Universe or we are not. Both are equally terrifying.

It was almost like the great afterlife conundrum. Do we want to know? Should certain questions be left unanswered? What would it mean if we were not alone in the universe?

To me it had always been an exciting possibility. I wanted there to be space travel and exploration, and to see the discovery of new species and cultures, even if it were a terrifying prospect for mankind. Take a moment to think of all the creatures on planet Earth that could maul, destroy or consume a person, from the bite of a tiny mosquito to the jaws of a shark or a lion, the poisons and stings of serpents and insects. There were so many terrible ways that Mother Nature could exterminate a human. Imagine what untold terrors might lie in wait for us on alien worlds, intelligent life forms that might look at us with disdain.

Susan had said she believed that on the inevitable return of the visitors she would be plucked from her home like corn in a field. She described it as a harvest. Could these powerful beings be reaping us, harvesting us like produce? What was it that we offered them? Surely not sustenance? Why had Susan used the word *harvest*? The word grew disturbingly in my mind like a thorny weed. I began to feel nauseous as my mind pondered the many dark ways a human being could be utilized in much the same way we misuse and mistreat animal life on our world.

I had recently read that from one slaughtered pig there are 185 different uses for the remains, from the obvious and consumable parts to more unlikely uses such as being used in bullets and washing powder. Could the same be done to us?

I welcomed arriving safely at my home, and that night as I lay in bed my thoughts whirled. Sleep was difficult to come by as it often is when dissecting a new case. Susan was a young and attractive woman, and it was melancholic to think of her self-inflicted lifestyle of solitude.

My mobile phone rang. It was nearly four in the morning. I own two phones; one for personal use and the other for professional engagements. This was my personal device. The number was withheld but I answered it, worrying that something bad had happened. I was greeted with a crackling line. I said hello and it blurted a sequence of clicks and sounds. Then it disconnected, and I was back in the silence of my bedroom illuminated by the phone's display.

I cannot for sure say if that call was related to the testimonial I was recording for Susan, but I found the timing to be unsettling. I have not received a call before or since of this nature. If it was connected, was I being tracked or followed? I did not want to become paranoid, but it did unnerve me. I finally fell into a sleep occupied by anxious and troubled dreams.

I awoke the next day with a mind swamped with the images of disaster in my peaceful county. As I sifted through my notes, I began to think, what if this was all real?

This was the most intelligent and articulate interviewee I had ever spoken to. I felt sure that, consciously or subconsciously, she believed her story to be true. I was troubled. Should I prepare myself for a cataclysmic catastrophe that would smash and burn for dozens of miles, polluting the sky, the Earth and sea for generations, killing thousands, potentially maiming tens of thousands more, and turn this peaceful land into a ground zero for one of the greatest disasters in modern history? There had been a great many alleged sightings of UFOs in and around the estuary, particularly over the last fifteen years. And Milford Haven is the second largest natural harbour in Europe, home to oil and gas refineries with gigantic oil tankers lumbering heavily up the estuary. The colossal ships carrying LNG (liquefied natural gas) dwarf the tugs and boats. Many within the community recognize the potential dangers of the refinery, but like everything that poses a potential threat we tend to carry on with our daily lives, forgetting the hazards of industry. Was Susan foreseeing a natural disaster? What if she was, in fact, a herald, a prophet who had seen a terrible disaster on the horizon? Could this be her real motivation? After all, if it was to be alien-induced, why would they show this to Susan? Were they testing her reaction to the desolation, measuring her emotional response? The imagery throughout of dead grandmothers, insects being pulled to pieces, shadowy men, is not uncommon in alien abductee cases. Do aliens experiment on us to determine our stage of evolution? Imagine, if you will, if a scientist was experimenting on an ape and the ape began to cry and begged for the scientist to stop hurting it; would we be kinder to it?

I was eager to hear more and while I waited for 4pm to arrive so we could continue into Susan's account I looked at the phenomenon of prophecy and prescience. Did Susan possess the same abilities such as Nostradamus, John the Baptist, Edgar Cayce and others who have claimed the foresight to see into the future and predict events? Was she using me as a mouthpiece?

Many of the words of these seers like Nostradamus can be interpreted after the event to fit what happened. But I do believe there is something going on here, particularly with more contemporary figures like the blind Bulgarian mystic Baba Vanga, who reportedly foretold 9/11, the 2004 Boxing Day tsunami, the Fukushima nuclear spill and the birth of ISIS, and had also made dire predictions for 2016 and beyond.

Dying in 1996 aged 85, she was known as "The Nostradamus from the Balkans" thanks to a purported 85% success rate, and has long been revered in Russia and Europe as a saint. Of the hundreds of predictions Vanga made over her half-century career as a celebrated clairvoyant, a large number alluded to natural and climate change-related disasters. She warned of melting polar ice caps and rising sea temperatures back in the 1950s, decades before anyone had heard of global warming. Her followers believe her vivid description of a "huge wave" that would descend on a "big coast, covering people and towns and causing everything to disappear under the water" was a reference to the 2004 tsunami and earthquake which claimed hundreds of thousands of lives across the Pacific Rim.

Can we dismiss such prophecies? Has Susan been privy to glimpses of the future of an impending disaster? I guess some local people have wondered what would happen if the refineries or an LNG ship exploded. Indeed, perhaps it's simply a case of "when" rather than "if".

I was restless for further details from Susan. Indeed, as each interview session continued, she never disappointed my inquisitiveness.

Susan: We buried Mog in the garden. Aunty thought maybe she had somehow eaten poison. Her eyes were covered in pus, her noise scabbed, and her poor little mouth surrounded by froth or spittle. We lay her in a shoe box, and I dug her in.

Aunty stood there wrapped in her big parka coat and scarf, coughing uncontrollably. She was really ill. It had come on so suddenly and my thought was that it must have something to do with those jellyfish-like creatures who had put their tendrils into Aunty and Mog, doing who knows what inside them. Extracting or pumping something? They weren't like anything on Earth.

My own health was suffering. Heavy painful periods, sweats, diarrhoea, vomiting, pains in my head, my neck, behind my eyes. I had always maintained a healthy diet, exercising with trips to the gym or a long run, but now I was becoming painfully skinny. I was losing my femininity as quickly as I felt I was losing my mind.

That day in the garden it dawned on me that the jellyfish creatures might be feeding off me every night. I was appalled. Was that why I was so ill? The Sian in my dream had said that it would be over, and I hoped she had meant it was over full stop. But for Aunty, I pleaded with her that she should go to the doctor. She agreed, though she dismissed it as just the flu.

That night there were no dreams, no nightmares, no shadow people or insects, just nothing. I did sleep a few hours, but I was terrified. Three nights in a row of that had been crippling enough.

Yes, I was severely depressed now, but I don't believe anyone could have helped me. These things were real to me. They would simply appear and disappear at a whim and do whatever they pleased, like a farmer walking into a chicken coop and taking out a hen for supper. They can enter our world through dreams, through visions, they prey upon you while you sleep, they control time, space, even our minds, and slip in and out unnoticed. I'm not going on ranting about it anymore. We *are* in the Matrix. I don't know if the Government knows but they're just as helpless as we are. It's not the insane who have got fiction and reality mixed up, it's all of us, they're just the ones who realise it.

Aunty went to the doctors, was told it was flu and given a week's sick note for work. Deep down I knew it wasn't. She looked so miserable; she had been such a beautiful woman but at this time she was grey and clammy.

However, things did get better. I lived my life day by day, fearful it would all come back, and it didn't, not for a long while. Aunty got a little better, so she said, and went back to work. I went back to university. Sian, Wendy and Karen ignored me. I sat at the back on my own in classes. I had invested so much time in our friendship and my study that I realised I had hardly any other friends. In hindsight I believe that was one blessing that can be taken from this. It meant fewer people would be hurt. Aunty was ill, Mog had died and Lennie was missing, though I knew they, they as in the visitors, the beings, had killed him.

My motivation for study was less though. I didn't put the effort in like I had before. I felt like a minor character in my own life story. I felt such a disconnect from reality. I walked with my head down and I started wearing a hoody, to hide my face.

Did I tell you that Sian, Wendy, Karen and I used to text each other what we were wearing so we could match? Sad, I know. Life is simpler with a hood covering your head. People tend to be distrustful of you, they give you a wider berth.

I had resumed my job in Haverfordwest, and was pulled in by my manager asking if I was OK. She said that I looked tired and ill, my appearance was shabby, and I was taking a noticeable amount of toilet breaks. My stomach pains, irritable bowels and irregular periods had not reduced since the visitors had left me alone.

My supervisor implied that if I was taking drugs I would be dismissed for misconduct. I was appalled. How quickly my life had turned for the worse. I had no friends and I was still not confident about talking to my parents. They would have had me sectioned. I was ill and falling apart, and everything and everyone around me was suffering. I apologised to her and said I was just ill, I did not advocate a drugs lifestyle or plan to use drugs. The poor woman asked me what advocate meant, she thought it was a fruit. I left the meeting with a smile and continued working.

Aunty just seemed to be constantly ill. The sparkle in her eyes had gone, she ate little and slept lots. She said I should go back to my parents, just for a while until she got better. I protested that I was happy living with her and that I wanted to take care of her. She said she wanted me gone at the end of the month; she just wanted to live alone and in peace.

I sat in my room sobbing because I thought what if Aunty had begun to believe that I had really brought these strange creatures into my life, and into her life. Had she been experiencing similar dreams and visions to me? Did she blame me for Mog's death? I was so weak and exhausted that I had no fight left in me. What was I to do, go and irritate Aunty even more by speaking about them? I just carried on quietly.

I left at the end of the month and moved in with my parents. By then Aunty had got worse, and was cold towards me, hardly speaking. I miss her so much. It's not my fault, it's not.

My parents, particularly my dad, were happy to have me back. My mother is rather cold in her approach whereas Dad is warmer and more interested in the lives of others. I hoped that moving away, being home safe, this truly was the end of it. It had been months and nothing seemed to have happened. I would not have been able to live with myself if this had all followed me back there and got my parents tangled up in it.

My parents' home was equidistant between Carmarthen and Haverfordwest, so it still served me well for university, but the journey to Haverfordwest for my work shifts after college were difficult. I had money, savings and an inheritance from Gran, but I wanted that for after my studying days so when I relocated for my vocation, my career, I would be able to afford a place to live, with decent furniture and so on. I had it all planned out. At that time, I just needed to snap into focus and get back on track.

I would get angry with Aunty, my friends and Adrian, but I thought soon enough I would have the life I wanted so badly, and I would start anew. New friends, colleagues, even relationships. Talking about that all now makes me feel so hollow, so empty. Life is just a huge joke. We place so much emphasis on insignificant things only for us to realise we have absolutely no control over our lives. We are ants in our anthill compared to these beings.

Things were quiet for months and I did start to gain traction. Things were getting better. Then I started to have a recurring dream.

In my dream I would be walking naked through a stream. It was night and the stream was tucked in by trees, I think it was a woodland. I could see around me as everything was bathed in a red light. I couldn't see the stars or moon, no street lights. I am out walking around in the countryside. I'm not cold or afraid, just walking through the stream, and then on to a stony bank and up upon a field. The grass is high, maybe it's a crop; it is up to my knees.

I stop, and I can see a beautiful fox sat there in the grass just staring at me, bathed in the red light. I can't see where the light is coming from. The fox's ears twitch back, and it stares right at me. I'm not afraid of the animal and I keep walking towards it. I feel like I know the fox, it sounds insane, but it seems familiar. As I get closer a huge whoosh comes from behind me and a giant owl, like the size of a man, swoops down and picks up the fox with its talons. The owl swoops around with the fox in its grip, the fox howling in fear and pain, and I feel blood spray all over me from above. I want to run and to scream but I can't. The fox is making an awful pitiful sound as the owl flies off into the woods. There is a blood-curdling scream, more like a person than an animal, and then silence.

I am compelled to keep walking, I need to get away from the owl, and as I walk through the field, bathed in the red light, I see a woman walk past me, as if in a trance. She is naked too. She seems older than me, maybe forty, maybe older. I follow her and soon see another woman, a woman in her sixties, then a young girl, no more than eleven or twelve. All of us walking, naked through the grass. I look around me and there are hundreds of us, different ages, ethnicity, body types, all heading in the same direction, walking naked, following each other like a herd of cattle. The red light intensifies and there is screaming and pleading, horrific sounds from the women in front of me and then I wake up.

I would wake up oddly calm, like I had been sedated. I had no feeling of pain or nausea, in fact I felt better. I had rationalised, as was the family way, that maybe this was my mind dealing with the trauma from earlier in the year. It seemed to be about vulnerability, but I usually felt at ease with it. It seemed perfectly natural, that hundreds of women would happily walk through the night, naked, through a field. It was only the women at the front who were panicking; those of us at the back were oblivious. The imagery of the fox was unsettling but not nearly as bad as bulbous creatures and horrific disasters. I felt like the fox was me and the owl was the visitors. I had been hunted and claimed by a superior predator, but if I hid it would not find me.

I soon found out my feelings of ease were mistaken. The dream was to become a nightmare, not just a nightmare but an actual living hell. Whatever it was out there had selected me and it was coming back.

I was driving back from Haverfordwest after a work shift. It had gone eleven at night and I would not be home for a least another fifteen minutes. The roads were quiet, with little traffic.

I had Radio 2 on through the car stereo and mid-song a terrible sound filled the car. I tried to turn off the radio, but the sound kept screeching through the car speakers. I pulled over into a lay-by and tried again. The sound was like an animal screaming and amongst that terrible noise was a clicking, almost like Morse code. I had until that point heard nothing like it before.

The sound stopped as suddenly as it had begun, and I sat there in my car, shaking. A car drove past and slowed down, and a man looked towards me. He stared at me blankly – not like he was concerned or worried, just staring – and I started the car up and drove home without any further incident.

A few nights later I was taking the same route home. I was worried so made an excuse to call home, to chat to my dad. He was still awake and happy to talk. I made up an excuse, asking something along the lines about a part of the course I was studying and if he thought my chosen essay was the right one to submit. We chatted as we drove and then the damn noise started again, again through the car speakers. I could hear Dad in the background asking if I was OK and what was happening. I tried to shout over the noise, the horrific sounds of something suffering and clicking as he shouted was I OK, had I had an accident. I pulled over and shut off the engine and turned off my phone, I turned off the Bluetooth, everything.

The noise stopped. I sat alone with my heart beating in my throat. I was a wreck. The phone rang and startled me, and it was Dad. He asked if I was OK, what had happened. He asked what that awful noise was. I asked him if he had heard the screeching and clicking and he said yes, it had come out of his phone too. I was so relieved that I cried with joy. Dad asked did I want him to come and get me, but I said no, I would be fine, and I would be home in ten minutes.

I hung up and I know it sounds silly but I knew this thing was back; I knew that it wasn't just me, that it wasn't in my head, that these things were interacting with our world. Now, today, I wish it was just all in my head, I wish I could just die, and all of this would die with me. Some days I think that would be the best thing to do. One day I will have the courage to just end it all. Suicide takes courage, more than I have at the moment.

A light appeared behind me and I started up the engine. I didn't want it to be that creepy-looking driver from the night before. The headlights appeared on the road behind and as I began to pull off the car stalled and the lights behind me rose vertically, silently and high into the night sky. It was several minutes before the car started again. They were close, always close, always watching.

They were my shepherds.

I drove home in a state of shock at what I had just seen. I imagined my self ploughing the car into a tree, ending my misery. I wondered if I would feel fear or remorse as I flew through the windscreen. I hoped it would be so quick that there would be no feeling at all. One minute I would be driving at speed, a flash and then nothing. The end of my suffering.

Why were they so blatant? Could everyone see them or was it just me? Was it them communicating through the car radio and phone? Were they talking to me, to each other, was it even a language? Dad had heard them.

When I got home, it had gone eleven thirty, Mother was on the phone and she was sat there quietly acknowledging the person on the other side of the phone. Dad was putting on his coat, his face was white. His eyes had welled up with tears. I asked what had happened.

Aunty, he told me, Aunty was in hospital, and she was riddled with cancer.

His sister was to be dead by the end of the week.

Celestial

For our struggle is not against flesh and blood, but against the rulers, against the authorities, against the powers of this dark world and against the spiritual forces of evil in the heavenly realms.
Ephesians 6:12

Over the many hours, the many days, this was the most emotional I'd seen her. Her beautiful green eyes welled up and her voice cracked as she told me of her aunt's final days. Her cancer had been diagnosed late, and it had ravaged her body like a swarm of locusts in a cornfield.

My immediate reaction was to reach out and offer comfort to this young woman, to offer her a hug of reassurance – my heart was breaking for her. But I knew that boundaries had to remain in place – a certain professionalism is required. It is difficult to sit back and watch my interviewees explain and describe their pain, fear, confusion, anger and grief. I am not insensitive or dismissive of the subject's feelings at all, but I am simply here to record, not act as a counsellor.

Had Susan created a fiction to disguise the pain of what had been happening to her – the missing dog, the loss of her friends, her slipping educational standards, a relationship break-up, the death of Mog and now her aunt? Had she cracked up, translating her emotions and pain into faceless men, bulbous insect-like creatures, end of the world scenarios and lights in the sky?

I wasn't sure. When Susan told me of the strange sounds in her car and on the phone a chill went through me; her description of the alien voices chattering in the night were not so dissimilar from the sounds on my phone. Was there a connection, or was this just coincidence? If this was real, I wasn't sure that I wanted to take it much further.

Susan asked for a break for a few days; she was exhausted

having been brought back to her aunt's death. It had been very distressing for her and I have not included the details in full, as such a personal family matter bears little relevance to Susan's story. I left her be, quietly leaving her flat as she sat surrounded in a haze of cigarette smoke and patchouli incense, with twinges of guilt for having pushed her too far.

She called me two days later inviting me back. I was relieved. As difficult as it was for Susan to recount her experiences I wanted to get to the end of them.

Session 8 of the interviews continues

Susan: I had been so tempted to speak to Dad the day of Aunt's funeral, tell him what was happening, ask him he could help it stop somehow, hide me away, protect me as a dad should. Mother was not one to open up to, so I saw little point in even discussing anything that was going to create trouble between us.

I stared at Dad at the crematorium and just wanted to fling my arms around him like I was a little girl again and tell him I was frightened. He had sat there, pale, gaunt and exhausted. His shock at the loss of his sister was palpable. He had lost his mother to cancer as well. Apart from myself and mother, all his family were now dead.

I then started to formulate an idea. To stop those around me dying, being hurt or being frightened I would ostracise myself. I would move out, live in Haverfordwest and live a solitary existence of work, study and then get through the nights. Maybe the visitors would move on, forget about me, find someone else. I thought I could become invisible if I lived in a built-up area. Another student, another young person living in a flat in Haverfordwest, another face in the crowd.

Dad was a stoic character, but he was devastated when I told him I was going to move back to Haverfordwest and live on my own. He held me close and sobbed into my ear that he just wanted his little girl home; he had said he had lost too many people that he loved, and he couldn't bear not to be around me.

Mother had said I was too old to be living at home though and it made sense that I lived local to my work. It was pretty much the same travel distance to university, and soon enough I would be leaving anyway to follow a career. My mother may seem cold, but she is practical in her thinking.

I picked out this flat and Dad helped me move in. He had been quiet, and he left after giving me the biggest hug ever. I hadn't been back living with him for long but we had reconnected, and as he had grown older, he had become more agreeable. When I feel alone or sad, scared or vulnerable I think of him and those few months we shared back home. I think about him all the time.

The next day he arrived unexpectedly with boxes galore of cooking utensils, a coffee maker, pots and pans, cups and crockery, a huge grocery shop, finest teas and coffees and more than I could ever eat in a year. He was sweating profusely and had carried all of it up the stairs. He had said it would set me up for life and when I would come home from work late at night I could think of him, or if I had a dinner party or guests I could pretend he was there helping me cook, getting in my way, adding too much salt. He was so thrilled to help. Every morning he said we would raise a toast to each other with our first cuppa of the day.

I love him so much.

Every time I make a cup of tea or cook myself a dinner, I do think of him. I never did have a dinner party or guests over. You are the first person other than my family or the landlady to ever step inside my flat. Maybe before this is all said and done, when you have my words, my testimony, before it's time to leave, I could cook you a supper. Only if it's OK. I don't want you to feel professionally obliged, only if you would like to. It would be nice to plate up for two.

I wasn't sure that by moving I would be safe. But you just have to hope that it will end, one day they will move along, and you will be free again.

That first night I had a peculiar and similar dream to the one with the fox and the owl.

I was alone, emerging from the woods, it was night time but the fields in front of me are bathed in red, like the light from a flare. From my viewpoint I couldn't see what was causing the light. It calmed me.

I had to cross the stream again and it was far deeper than it was before. It was up to my waist. I was naked again but this time I was not me as I am now, but as a little girl, maybe nine or ten years old.

I stumbled through the freezing cold stream. I could feel the biting of the cold water, then I scrambled up a stony bank and stood and gazed upon a field of tall grass, illuminated in the red glow.

I looked for the fox, the fox was my friend, but it wasn't there. I heard a screech behind me, it was the great big owl. I was much smaller as a child and knew that I was easy pickings for it, so I had to keep moving. I had to get into the deep grass and hide, to find someone to help me.

As I walked through the long stems of grass, I saw a naked woman walking towards me. I walked quickly towards her – women in the field were not the ones to be fearsome of, the more of us that huddled together the safer we would be.

As I got closer, I saw that the woman was my mother, strolling nude through the grass. She seemed a good ten or fifteen years younger than she is now. Her face was calm, almost content, a rarity in the real world. She walked past me and casually took my hand and took me forwards with her. Up ahead were the silhouettes of two other women. I knew if two could become four then the odds of safety increased. We reached them and I was relieved to see the two other women were my grandmother and my aunty, both younger, both so much healthier than when I last saw them. Both very much alive.

They both looked at me calmly, a slight smile on my gran's face, and together the four of us walked through the field, the red light growing brighter as we walked.

Then I woke up. Oddly calm again.

My immediate reaction was to question whether any others in the family had experienced these visitations. Were the visitors interested in our family tree, our DNA, our genetic make-up? No one had ever mentioned it. Gran and Aunty were dead and there was no way I was ever going to broach this with my mother. She could have had me committed. And my thinking was that if I ended up in care, medicated to oblivion, I could become a prisoner of the creatures, trapped in the dungeon of my body. If I was on the loose, so to speak, I could hope they went away or at the very least hope I could find something out that could stop the terrorizing or find the right people to help me. I detested the idea of being seen by some doctor listening to my rants, a mad woman talking about aliens and dead dogs, giant owls and naked women in fields. They would lock me up for sure.

I ask you now, when is a dream just a dream? How can we really tell what is real and what we created? You could be in a coma right now, thinking, believing, creating a world where you are interviewing people for your book. This is a question I want to ask of you because this next episode defies everything I have ever known. It was beyond all comprehension.

A few weeks later I had come home from work, it had gone a quarter past ten, at night. I had some supper, ran a bath, put on my PJs and sat right here on the sofa to do some study with a cup of tea. Now, many of these occurrences seem to be dreams or nightmares, often when I have gone to bed, but this instance was decidedly different.

I think I must have nodded off while I was revising.

I found myself outside, in the street. I was still in my pyjamas, barefooted. It was chilly outside, but the air was still. I thought to myself, *"Why am I out here?"* It wasn't pitch black as the street was lit with the street lamps and lights coming from houses. It was an odd feeling, but this was an altogether different experience from my Christmas experience. This seemed... more real.

I thought about walking back to the flat, but I could see someone at the end of the street. It looked like a woman just stood there looking at the sky. She appeared to have a big coat on, a cloak. I thought to myself, was she OK? Why is she stood in the street just looking up? I walked towards her and I felt obliged to look up too.

There was a sky full of stars, but they were all red, moving, swirling like a million embers. The sky was not black but more of a red mist with pinpoints of bright red moving lights. A dull red moon hung in the sky, revolving slowly. The sight of it left me aghast but also curious. I knew that I had to be dreaming, but this was so vivid, and my actions were lucid. I was very conscious about my actions and thoughts. I looked back down the street and the woman at the end was walking towards me, slowly. Clothed in a red coat that touched the ground, her face draped in a hood or cowl that made me wonder if this actually was a woman or not. It was more like a monk, dressed in a deep red.

My heart started to beat so hard that I knew I had to go. Whoever this was it was not going to be good. As it got closer, I could hear her making that strange awful screeching and clicking noise, like I had heard in the car, quieter though than it had been through the car speakers. I started walking back to the flat, walking as fast as I could, wanting to run but compelled to make sure I didn't step on anything on the ground that could cut my feet.

I walked back through the front entrance, making sure I closed it firmly behind me, and I took the flight of stairs two or three steps at a time. I got to my floor and I had left my flat door wide open, the kitchen light was still on, and I closed the door behind me, locked it and put up the chain. I kept thinking, *I will wake up in a minute.*

I sat back down on the sofa, and my books and tea were still there. I stood up and distinctively made the decision to make a fresh cup of tea. I checked my phone, even sat back down with my tea. When was I going to wake up?

I looked out of the window on to the street below. Cars were parked on the street, the sleepy town bathed in the light of a red full moon. I was so bewildered that I checked my phone to see if some weather phenomena or astronomical event was taking place that I was not aware of.

It was a little before 11pm so I texted my dad asking if he was OK. He texted me back saying he and Mother were watching a movie, and he asked if I had a good day in work. I still have these texts to this day. I took a series of pictures from my window, of the red gloomy street, part of me was tempted to go back out and photograph the moon and sky but I was afraid of the red woman out in the street. You can see the pictures I took, and there was nothing in them at all that corroborates what I witnessed.

I sat there perplexed. Had I sleepwalked? Was I having a hallucination from carbon monoxide or something similar? I quickly opened the window and peered out again into the red world. I was tempted to knock on a neighbour's door to ask, was everything OK? Was I OK?

I needed the loo and headed off and sat there, scrolling through my newsfeed, checking social media to see if anyone else was experiencing this. I walked back into the living room and there it was. I screamed.

The red figure was stood there in my living room. Its cloak billowed silently around her, like she was standing in a vortex, and I stood there, watching, frozen.

Its hood was off, and I looked at what I could describe as a woman, an alien woman. Feminine but clearly not human. She had some type of tubes protruding out of a black mask across her mouth and she was making that awful screeching and clicking sound. Her nose was incredibly small and pointed, and she had red thick unkempt hair untidy over a large smooth forehead. The top of her head bigger and out of proportion to the rest of her face. It was her eyes, huge dark eyes that terrified me. I have seen those eyes before on shows and films about aliens but these were not grey but red. The eyes were unblinking, almond-shaped, taking up a third of her face.

Those eyes were more insect than human.

It moved to me and touched my hand with a red claw-like hand and I screamed loudly. I felt cold and electricity shoot through my skin. Then there was a rushing in my ears, my scream turned to silence, my body went numb, and then it was as if the world stopped spinning and time froze. An awfully unnerving experience, terribly difficult to describe.

The thing, the red woman, left through the now wide-open front door. I stood there, static clicking around me, my skin goose-bumped, my arm hair on end and I was wetting myself.

You are no doubt waiting for the *and I woke up* part. I didn't wake up. I was awake for two solid days without sleep. As soon as I got my bearings and stopped panicking I ran and closed the front door and locked and chained it again. I ran to the window and looked out into the street. It was normal, just street lights illuminating the street and cars. The street was empty and no sign of the red woman. No red mist, red stars or a spinning red moon. Just a normal world.

I sat back down on the sofa and sobbed. You must hear this a lot in your accounts, Mr Davies, but I thought that I had gone mad, that I had been spiked with drugs or was part of a horrendously elaborate joke or experiment.

With your hauntings and ghosts they are usually set in a house, there are the same kind of events, there's a history to unearth, clues to be solved. Whatever is happening to me there's no way to source it, to connect the dots or unearth a Rosetta Stone that helps you make sense of this. I wish this was a haunting.

I'd leave the house, get some sage, say some prayers, sprinkle some holy water and call a fucking exorcist, and sell my shitty ghostly experience to the trash magazines by the supermarket checkouts.

This is nothing like that, this is real, and it comes and goes whenever it wants as your brain desperately stretches and snaps trying to figure out just what the hell it is experiencing. How can we comprehend things we cannot possibly relate to? I have no idea what happened, why it happened and for what purpose, if any. They, I don't know if they are the same species, us from the future, or different, working with or against each other, but they can manipulate time, thoughts, actions, our perceptions, our physical world, our technologies, our memories, and none of it makes any or will ever make any sense to us.

What happened next terrified me more than everything that happened before combined. I'm still terrified.

Gavin, you must help me, please you must. I don't want to live anymore. I just can't take anymore.

Bygone

They're gonna put it down, Right on the strip
They're gonna put it down, On the Vegas strip
They're gonna put it down, And step outside
Into the lights, Right outta that ship
Saying hi!
The Pixies, *The Happening*

Susan had lost control of her stoic approach and begged me
frantically to make it all stop. I stood up, and went to the
kitchenette and made tea for us both. She is a vegan, never has
milk, and the more I heard the more I understood her reasons.
As the kettle bubbled and the steam rushed out, I heard her
sobbing behind me, and I felt so desperately inept. A cup of
tea, a reassuring word, advice on psychological trauma would
not ease the suffering this young woman has experienced. I had
experienced this with the home I had owned, the house that
would become the *Haunted: Horror of Haverfordwest*. There is
little to compare to the feelings of inadequacy in the presence of
something so unfathomable and powerful.

Her account was so incredibly detailed, with texts and times,
working patterns and university classes to confirm her comings
and goings; she provided everything and anything she could to
prove that these events were happening. She was paranoid that
I would think her to be a fraud.

I made the tea and brought it to her. She dragged deeply on
a cigarette, her face wet from tears. The room filled with the
smoky apparitions of apprehension.

I told her what I was about to say could possibly upset
her, but I had a duty of care, and care I did, and there were
professional, medically-trained people who would be willing to

help, to offer sensitive counsel at the very least. I have conducted enough study across the years to understand there are very real and common psychological imbalances that can make terrifying imaginary events seem very real, and that there are good people out there who want to support a person through the trauma. I said that was not to say that what she had experienced was *not* real. I explained that I too had to get help with my own mental well-being when I was subjected to a terrifying paranormal ordeal.

She fired a barrage of vulgarities at me. I let her vent her feelings, her anger. I did not take it personally as her upset could be in part due to it simply being the first time Susan had ever told anyone. I believed after many sessions of interviews that I was in no harm, and if I did feel threatened I would just leave. I do not get paid for my time or for my expenses at the interview stage, and if I feel that I may come into physical harm or if the interview is not worth further time or needs no further inquiry then I walk away.

I allowed her to continue with her furious rhetoric while I stared unflinchingly into my tea.

She stopped and I looked at her. She was sat there, sobbing into the cradle of her arm. Between sobs she asked me, repeatedly, did I believe her? I replied, honestly, I didn't know. I told her it scared me. I told her, if there was a way I could help her to have a normal life then I would but if this was real, that if alien beings were that intensely focused on her, that I doubted there was anything I could do to assist. I asked her sincerely, would having her account published help? Maybe it was too much for her to suffer through. Did we need to do this? Did she need to do this?

She looked up and smiled and said that the book had to be written because other women, other people would know this was real, would know what was happening to them, and at least they could band together, offer support to each other, watch over each other, maybe all go to the government or media and say this is all real, it's happening to all of us, you need to protect your people.

Susan stood up and asked me to follow her. She walked down the corridor towards the loo and her bedrooms. I was confused as to what she wanted. I was certainly not going to follow a young woman into her bedroom. I had used her loo several times during the visits but she had always had her bedroom doors closed. She opened one of them and turned on the light.

It wasn't a bedroom. It was a room with wall to wall research. Newspaper clippings, sketches, paintings and drawings I could only assume were made by her, dozens of books and DVDs all based on the subject of aliens and alien abductions.

Her pictures showed fields and naked women standing amongst the tall grass, lights in the sky, lights following a car, faceless sticklike men, bulbous creatures with tendrils attached to a black cat which I could only assume to be the doomed Mog, and of course the red woman with the gigantic insect-like eyes. Books covered the tables and bookcases, from von Däniken to Whitley Strieber, from Timothy Good to Jenny Randles, and every possible avenue of alien research in between. She was deeply embedded in the mythology of UFO and alien abduction.

The vastness of it all, the amount of detail, staggered me. I felt the room swirl around me.

Dumbfounded, I sat back down in the living room and Susan followed me back. She brought with her two large scrapbooks, bursting with bits of paper and bookmarks. She opened one and showed me all the reports and research that was available for the 1975 to 1982 Welsh UFO Triangle case. She said the Pembrokeshire area was prone to such events and maybe in amongst all the reports there was a kernel of truth that would explain or connect the events she was suffering through.

For those not familiar with the details, here is a brief synopsis of what occurred. The events that materialised in the mid-

1970s in Pembrokeshire are shrouded in conspiracy, conjecture, rumours, with retractions of key witness statements and new evidence being supplied nearly forty years later. What had happened and did it bear any relevance to Susan's case? This is for you, the reader, to judge. Should you wish to do your own research I have sourced the material I have used.

We shall return to Susan after this brief interval for her own horrific, shocking finale.

I have used the following documents to piece together a brief abridgment of the events. *The Welsh Triangle* by Peter Paget (1979), *The Dyfed Enigma* by Pugh and Holiday (1981), *The Uninvited* by Clive Harold (1979) and *The Alien World* Volume 1 (an Orbis Publication, 1984), and the excellent reporting and archiving that was conducted by the local paper, the *Western Telegraph*.

UFOs up in the sky and on the ground. Cars pursued by orange footballs, glowing cigars hovering above schools. Discs flying into solid rock and vanishing between sliding doors. Silver suited entities with no faces stalking across fields and staring through cottage windows. Mysteriously malfunctioning cars, television and radio sets. Visits from sinister aliens with psychic powers. The teleportation of entire herds of cattle. Such, if the reports are to be believed, are just some of the extraordinary events that occurred not in some far-off land but in peaceful, homely, Wales and not at some distant point in time but as recently as the spring of 1977.

The Story of the Welsh Triangle – The alien world 1984

Pembrokeshire is the most westerly county in Wales, extending into the Irish Sea. It's framed by all manner of beautiful beaches, coves and bays, and the picturesque Preseli Hills. For such a large geographical area, the population is sparse.

The industrial area of the Milford Haven estuary has experienced UFO sightings for decades. Reports have been filed for lights and objects where no explanation seemed possible. The lifeboat has been turned out for lights which have never been identified, and aircraft crossing the area have also made curious observations. Some people dismissed them as military in nature – there is a Royal Air Force and United States Air Force presence, there were Cold War submarine tracking operations, tank and helicopter training grounds, to say nothing of the Napoleonic and First and Second World War outposts along the coastline.

There had been sightings before the 1970s. In 1959, a gentleman walking down Charles Street in the town of Milford Haven spotted a strange object flying overhead. It was said to be about 50 feet (15 metres) above the ground and moving on a downward track. It was described as *enormous*, around 150 feet in diameter (46 metres), metallic grey in colour, travelling quite slowly. It was circular and revolving, and disappeared behind the Tabernacle church and down towards the harbour. He never saw the craft again.

Another man recalled how when he was a young lad he and his sister had to make their way to school through a field and a wood situated in Freystrop. One evening they saw a bright yellow object around the size of a bicycle wheel which at first they thought to be a balloon. It was floating amongst the trees, and was moving backwards and forwards like a pendulum at least six feet each way. The children had run home terrified. Although they continued to use the same route, they were then usually accompanied by their grandfather.

But these minor reports were nothing compared to what would descend upon the county in the mid-1970s.

In 1975 and 1976, Haverfordwest and its surrounding area became a hub for UFO sightings. One lady claimed while walking her dog on the racecourse that she heard a humming noise above her. It had been misty that night, and she said above her was a great big light. She panicked at first thinking it was a helicopter making an emergency landing and would land on top of her and her dog. She dragged the petrified pet away, and watched as the anomalous light hovered a few feet off the ground and suddenly blazed a sequence of coloured lights at her. She ran, dragging the poor hound with her. When she got to the safety of the road the object, the sound, the lights had all gone.

Just after Christmas 1975, two UFOs landed near Haverfordwest. The first one looked like a glowing reddish ball which slowly descended into a wood. There were six or seven witnesses, and the next day they organized themselves into a search party to look for traces of the objects, but none were found.

Two weeks later a similar object was seen hovering above the grass in a field. The *Western Telegraph* newspaper stated that witnesses saw a red ball and fled. The report continued,

> *two youths fled in terror from a field on a Clarbeston Road farm last week when they saw a strange ball of light shoot off into the night from right in front of them. A fifteen-year-old and a seventeen-year-old said they could see the light shining through the hedge around twenty yards away. It rose in front of the tractor and disappeared.*

Soon the reports were flooding in and by 1977 they were on a scale that prompted local UFO researcher Randall Jones Pugh to comment that the entire *country was in for a spate of such incidents.*

One of the key events that alerted the public that something extraordinary was taking place was the alleged encounter made by a group of children from Broad Haven primary school.

The first sighting took place during the lunch break when a group of boys aged between nine and eleven who were playing football noticed an unfamiliar object in another field close by. It was at ground level, and was partly obstructed by trees and bushes so that the boys could only discern its upper portions. They believed what they were looking at was a UFO. Some of the boys, excited and startled, rushed into the school with the news.

Others came to see, until approximately 15 children witnessed the object.

They described the object as being *as long as a coach* (bus), maybe a bit longer. One description was of two saucers stacked one against the other to make a dome with a round *ashtray* added to make a smaller dome on top. One boy claimed to see three or four windows on the edge while others thought the number was closer to ten. Lights were said to be seen on top of the object and one witness reported the light as red. The object was said to have a door on the side with a ramp or platform extending from it while some but not all said they heard a humming noise emanating from the craft. Six of the children claimed they saw entities near the object.

"We saw something come out of it, it had a helmet," described one while another described it as, *"A silver man with spiked ears,"* and another, *"He wasn't a very tall person, and he didn't look very nice either."*

The children watched the object for some 20 minutes. Two of them went to tell the headmaster, but he was not interested at the time. At 2pm the children went back to class to remerge for break at 3.30pm. The object could not be seen from the earlier vantage point, but the more adventurous pupils continued looking and saw the object appear from behind a bush. This time they reported that the object *was tugging an object which was silver* and then again disappeared behind another bush.

Soon the sightings began in earnest with the county of Pembrokeshire gripped by a hysteria fuelled by the coverage of local and national media.

A twelve-year-old boy from Herbrandston, Pembrokeshire, claimed he was chased by a man from outer space. He described being chased from the sewage plant by a man in a boiler suit and visor. Was this a misidentified sewage worker or alien life form, no one really knew, however, the boy's family also claimed to have seen a strange aerial phenomenon before the youngster's ordeal and had seen a round ball of fire. The luminous ball hung stationary at no great altitude. The witnesses stated that after 24 years of living by the estuary they had never seen anything like it before.

On 10ᵗʰ February 1977 two twelve-year-old boys saw a UFO in a field near Haverfordwest Grammar school (Tasker-Milward). It was a blue flashing light seen at around 130 feet (40 metres). One boy claimed to have thrown a stone at it whereupon it took off, and as it did an orange cigar-shaped object of about 16 feet (five metres) long materialised beneath it, hovered for a while and then vanished.

During the morning of 16ᵗʰ February, a 13-year-old schoolboy of Pembroke Dock saw a bright metallic object hovering over Pembroke School as he arrived in the morning. He claimed the object had a dome in the middle which was dark grey but flashed to a dazzling white every five seconds. He said it *resembled a plate with a burnt fried egg on it*. Around the rim of the *plate*, it had green, yellowish lights and what seemed to be retro rockets. He said he *was sure it wasn't a helicopter or weather balloon.*

John Petts, the then famous artist, reported to BBC Wales from his home in Ferryside, Carmarthenshire, that he had witnessed a UFO manoeuvre over the estuary of Ferryside, in March 1977. He had been working late, at around 1am, and believed he saw a strip of light with a bright light on either end. He said it was pale like the moon. The object was shaped liked a *weaver's shuttle* and was by his determination to be a mile away and over 40 feet (twelve metres) long.

On 13ᵗʰ March, a teenager aged 17 saw a UFO at around 9pm. It was a glowing light with an orange halo around it. Half an hour later he saw a dome-shaped UFO of about 20 feet (six metres) high and stopped to look at it. He claims a tall man approached, wearing a semi-transparent suit and some type of spaceman's helmet. The teen was so afraid that he said, *"I just took a swing at it and ran away."*

During the early hours of 7th April 1977, a 64-year-old gentleman woke at approximately 4.45am disturbed by a strange orange light pulsating in his bedroom. The source of the light was from outside, and when he went to look, he could see that the sky was orange. He reported seeing two silvery-coloured objects. The first was like a very large Easter egg and four feet (1.2 metres) in diameter, and was swinging back and forth a little above the chimneys of the house opposite. "I saw a man in a silvery boiler suit about 40 feet (twelve metres) above my window. He was at least seven feet tall (two metres) hanging stationary on a level with the *Easter egg*." Its attitude was in the position of a free fall parachute jumper. It hung motionless in the sky, face downwards for about 25 minutes. The *Easter egg* then moved up above roof level and glided away sideways as did the figure.

On 19th April, an owner of a local seaside hotel was going to bed at around 2am when she was disturbed by a strange humming sound. At first, she took it for the central heating. A flash outside her window caused her to look outside. She saw a bluish light circling around, pulsating as it went. Taking out her binoculars, she could see an oval object resting on the ground and near it two figures in *"whitish plasticised clothing like boiler suits"*. She claimed the people had no faces.

All these sightings (over 45 such reports were recorded in 1977) were no doubt bewildering to the people who witnessed them but couldn't compare to the terror experienced by one family, the Coombs from Broad Haven, Pembrokeshire.

Mr Coombs and his wife lived with their five children in a cottage on Ripperston Farm on the coast near Broad Haven. Mr Coombs was the head herdsman, one of three men responsible for looking after the farm. There are many accounts in books, news reports and from people at the time to what really happened to the family, so the most probable version has been selected. However, please note that accuracy cannot be guaranteed with dealing with such an account.

Clive Harold stated in the Introduction to *The Uninvited*:

> *The story you are about to read is true, though you will doubt it.*
> *This is a story of an ordinary family caught up in the extraordinary,*
> *for whom the impossible came possible, the unbelievable believable,*
> *science fiction became fact... They no longer worry whether their*
> *story is believed or not, for they know the truth... They hope that*
> *others – the authorities in particular – may profit from its telling.*
> *They feel – as maybe we all should – that we ignore such phenomena*
> *at our peril.*

The first major event to strike the family was on 16th April 1977. Mrs Coombs, the mother, was driving home one evening with three children. Her ten-year-old son who was sat in the back seat reported a strange light in the sky. It was said to be around the size of a rugby ball, luminous, yellowish with a hazy grey light underneath and a torchlight beam shining down from it.

The son warned his mother that the light had U-turned and was now following them. The object caught up with the car and travelled alongside it, matching the car's speed, at which point the car lights began to dim. Closer to the house the car's engine cut out and Mrs Coombs had to freewheel the rest of the way back to the safety of the house. Mrs Coombs ran in to get her husband, and he and the eldest son came out just in time to see the UFO heading out to sea.

Mrs Coombs would go on to see another UFO from her kitchen window. It was about 20 feet (six metres) in diameter, and hovered about one metre off the ground. The object was said to be silvery in colour, had an antenna and a tripod undercarriage. It was said to have taken off and moved towards the sea, leaving burn marks on the ground.

Two of the younger children believed they had seen three UFOs in the sky, circular in shape with domes. One was gauged to be around 50 feet (15 metres) from above the ground and from it a ladder was lowered where a silver-suited figure was said to be climbing down. The UFO dropped a fluorescent box-like object on to the grass underneath. The children claimed they had looked for the box, but it had apparently disappeared.

On 22nd April 1977, Mr and Mrs Coombs were watching a late-night movie on TV. They had said that interference had been particularly bad that night. Around 11.30pm, Mrs Coombs became aware of a glow outside the sitting room window. An hour later Mr Coombs claimed to see a face at the window. *"It was a man – but a terrible size,"* he said of the intruder. He estimated the height of the figure to be seven feet (two metres), and he was wearing a white suit. He believed the face of the being was hid behind a black visor.

The police were called but they found no trace of an intruder, just a frightened family.

Around three weeks later a similar creature was sighted by the Coombs' eight-year-old twins. They described, while playing in a field, a similar being to what their parents had seen. The humanoid was dressed in silver with a black head and walked past them disappearing, having walked through a barbed wire fence.

Of all the events that were reported from Ripperston Farm the most astonishing was the seemingly supernatural movement of cattle. On several occasions, Mr Coombs found that the cattle, sometimes only one or two of the bovine beasts but sometimes the complete herd, had vanished from the yard. On one occasion he received an angry telephone call from a neighbouring farmer asking him to come for his herd. Mr Coombs asserted that the animals had been properly secured, and to have moved would have meant all the animals walking past the cottage in which the family lived, yet neither he nor his wife had seen or heard anything.

On another occasion he reported that there was no earthly

way that there had been enough time from when he had last seen the cattle to move such a distance. The cattle were said to have been so startled and disturbed that the milk yield decreased.

Electrical items at the farm were constantly suffering and having to be replaced. The events had highly malevolent influences on mechanical objects. Mr Coombs reported he had to replace his car five times during 1977, and an even higher rate of television sets. Light bulbs often exploded, and the TV and radio sets often would experience high levels of interference before breaking. The family's electricity bill was so high that they asked the electricity board to inspect the meters, and no fault was found.

Before their rise, trending in the zeitgeist of popular culture through films and comics, the men in black had been seen for many decades, worrying and threatening those with claims of UFO sightings and encounters of the first to fourth kind. In ufology, a close encounter is an event in which a person witnesses an unidentified flying object. This terminology and the system of classification behind it were first suggested in astronomer and UFO researcher J. Allen Hynek's 1972 book *The UFO Experience: A Scientific Inquiry.*

Close encounters of the first kind are classified as visual sightings of an unidentified flying object, seemingly less than 500 feet away, that show an appreciable angular extension and considerable detail.

Second Kind: A UFO event in which a physical effect is alleged. This can be interference in the functioning of a vehicle or electronic device; animals reacting; a physiological effect such as paralysis or heat and discomfort in the witness; or some physical trace like impressions in the ground, scorched or otherwise affected vegetation, or a chemical trace.

Third Kind: UFO encounters in which an animated creature is present. These include humanoids, robots, and humans who seem to be occupants or pilots of a UFO.

Close Encounters of the Fourth Kind is a UFO event in which a human is abducted by a UFO or its occupants.

Fifth Kind: A UFO event that involves direct communication between aliens and humans.

Sixth Kind: Death of a human or animal associated with a UFO sighting/Alien encounter.

And finally, the Seventh Kind: The creation of a human/alien hybrid, either by sexual reproduction or by artificial scientific methods.

Sinister (unearthly) men in black made their appearance. One day an unusual car was said to have driven up silently to the cottage. The car contained two men who were remarkably similar in appearance. One emerged from the car, immaculately dressed in a neat black suit and gleaming shoes. The visitor had been examining the cattle yard when a neighbour spotted him, yet uncannily he appeared next to her, and he asked for the whereabouts of Mrs Coombs. He was described as speaking in a foreign accent and as having something *alien* about him. He possessed *large, penetrating blue eyes which seemed to go right through her and examine her thoughts.*

The report continued with the eldest of the Coombs sons, who was in the neighbouring cottage at the time but was too frightened by the visitors to open the door to them. Instead he bolted the door and hid upstairs.

The neighbour was pressed for further information by the peculiar individual, but she claimed that he knew the answers before she uttered them. Then he asked for directions to their next location and the two men set off in their strange vehicle. A few moments later Mrs Coombs arrived in the car and had not seen the strange vehicle or its occupants. Please note that there was no turn-off on the lane, and Mrs Coombs claims not to have passed the car on her way home.

There were other alleged incidents of dark-shaped prowlers

in the yard, black shapes moving through the house and almost poltergeist-like activity in and around the cottage. One of the family claimed that a disembodied hand had left a terrible burn mark on her arm.

It should be noted that the incidents on the farm and surrounding area were not the first ones that Mrs Coombs had reported. Sometime before coming to Ripperston, the family had been dwelling in a caravan at nearby Pembroke Dock. Strange events and manifestations occurred there. Every evening, from inside the caravan, Mrs Coombs could see the life-size apparition of the Virgin Mary who was wearing a white dress. The vision was wearing a rosary tied around her waist and was holding the child Jesus. Later the apparition would morph into Jesus on his own. The figure would remain for up to half an hour. Once word travelled, sightseers, hoping to catch a glimpse of the phenomena, would visit the site. It is alleged that the owner of the caravan had it destroyed to stop the attention it was getting. Was Mrs Coombs prone to fantasy, wanting to be important? Or did she have a gift?

I was concerned that Susan had built her stories on these distant cases, taking them too much to heart. It was hard to get to the truth of them, surrounded as they were with misleading statements and mischievous inventions. My own belief is that there is a kernel of truth in almost every story. Every myth has a seed, a beginning, that takes root and later blossoms into something fantastical.

I asked Susan if she believed this was what was happening to her. She said some of her experiences were similar, like the faceless men and orange globes in the sky, but she had done more research into this than I would ever know and believed some of it was based on fact. She had contacted and spoken to people that most investigators had not even considered, and she believed there was a fragment of truth in it all that would connect that time period to the present.

She closed the large volume on the Pembrokeshire events of decades past and sighed deeply. She took out the second scrapbook and placed in on the coffee table in front of me, and began rolling a cigarette.

She said she had dedicated her life to looking for answers, to find a way to escape the attentions of the visitors. She had consumed books, videos, newspaper reports, online reports, anything she could to find out why this was happening to her. Her voice trembled as she told me, while she tried to hide the terror in her voice. And it wasn't only her, there were others that she knew were experiencing this, a great many others, hundreds if not more, even people from here in Pembrokeshire.

She stared deep into my eyes and said what she was about to tell me would terrify me beyond anything I had ever dealt with in my life. She said no matter what happened to her that I must publish the account; I must let the world know something inhuman was happening to people all over the world.

Her hands trembled almost uncontrollably as she opened the second large book.

Harvest

We cut the throat of a calf and hang it up by the heels to bleed to death so that our veal cutlet may be white; we nail geese to a board and cram them with food because we like the taste of liver disease; we tear birds to pieces to decorate our women's hats; we mutilate domestic animals for no reason at all except to follow an instinctively cruel fashion; and we connive at the most abominable tortures in the hope of discovering some magical cure for our own diseases by them.

George Bernard Shaw, *Man and Superman*

Susan: The whole reason I have reached out to you and asked for help is not so you can label me with a bunch of psychological issues but so you can tell the world the truth to what is happening to women just like me. Women here in Pembrokeshire, in Wales and across the world.

My family has a background in psychiatric study and medicine, and I know well enough what are clear-cut mental health issues, what can be deemed real and what can be delusional. I have read hundreds of witnesses' accounts from all over the world and people are experiencing the same thing. Black women, white women, women of all races, ages, sexual preference, religions, backgrounds – these things, these aliens, they do not care, they are harvesting us. With some they take enough not to be noticed, leaving people drained and desperately ill, riddled with cancer and other diseases, and in some cases taking their lives.

Think about how many people simply vanish into thin air. Hundreds of thousands of people simply vanishing without a trace. Normal people heading home, never to be seen again, their car found parked up in a field. Campers disappearing during trips to the wilds only to have bears and serial killers blamed for their removal from this world. There are people that are plucked from their beds, from their lives; some have been harvested or worse still cultivated for a far more sickening purpose.

I have seen it. I have witnessed it. What I am about to tell you is genuine, real, not a fabrication, everyone needs to know what is really going on in our world, what is happening to us. It explains why some people feel so sickly, so drained, so ill all the time.

I was driving back from my parents; I had gone up for Sunday dinner. I hadn't stayed that long as I said I was deep into my studies. I had lied of course, I was on a final warning for poor attendance and lack of motivation. My tutors were saddened that a star pupil could so quickly fall from grace. I was constantly exhausted, distracted and my behaviour was erratic and impatient. I was surviving on around three to four hours' sleep a night if that. Energy drinks, coffee and cigarettes became my best friend during the long nights. Not that it mattered being awake. The red woman had proven that by just walking into my flat.

As far as I was concerned, they would come and visit me whenever they chose. I wanted to be awake, so I knew it had happened and maybe somehow spot a weakness, find a way to hurt them, tell them to back off, to get out of my life. I didn't want to miss a thing, an opportunity to escape this. Maybe if I fought, they would see me as problematic, not worth the bother. Then again, they could kill me as easily as they had Lennie.

I was staring at the road ahead, it was getting dark, around 8pm. It was the same road I had driven a hundred times, the only road, hills to the left, and woodland and fields to my right. I was just immersed in the headlights on the road, running on autopilot, some random radio station playing when I instinctively hit the brakes.

The car screeched to a halt. I was lucky there was no one behind me as they would have crashed straight into the back of me. The road was empty, no car lights behind or in the distance.

I had braked as sat in the road was a beautiful fox. Its eyes illuminated green by the headlights of the car, its fur, beautifully healthy, full and red, its chin and chest brilliantly white. I stared at it, hypnotised by its elegance and its beauty.

As I stared at the fox, I was almost unaware that the radio had become distorted, crackling with interference until the crackling became an intense screeching accompanied by the clicking noises I had heard previously. Before I could panic, realise it was back, the car was bathed in an intense red light.

The fox stared at me; it looked like it was crying, tears welling up in its eyes and then the car lights faded, and the red light intensified until all I could see was red.

Then I was gone.

As vivid as I am speaking to you now and more intense than before, I found myself stepping out of some woodland. The sky was red, everything was bathed in that red light, that glow and I was naked. I crossed a stream, stony pebbles sticking into my feet, the coldness sharp and biting. In the dreams I felt I was being drawn along but this time I was in control of my actions. I knew I had to get to the tall grass as I knew something unwelcome was in the woodlands behind. The owl. I wrapped my arms around myself shivering. I knew I would die out here if I didn't find clothes or shelter soon.

As I scrambled up the stony bank of the stream, my hands cold, covered in mud, nails filled with dirt, I heard a screech from somewhere deep in the woods and I rushed up and into the field. The fox was sat there and when it saw me it darted into the long grass. I quickly followed it. The idea that a fox was helping me sounds absurd but in relation to everything else it seemed perfectly natural.

I knew I had to find the road. My mind was a little hazy as I thought maybe I'd had a car crash; I even thought I was dead, that I was a ghost. Nothing quite made sense, but I didn't have the calmness I had during or after the dreamlike states where I had been here before. I was cold, scared and could feel myself dying.

There in the field was a shape, I ran towards it. I shouted, *"Hello."* It was a naked black lady, somewhat older than I, with tight short black hair just walking along. I ran up to her and she grabbed hold of me, chattering frantically in a language I could not understand. We held each other close, the warmth of her body reassuring against the cold of the night. I didn't know how to reply so said, *"Let's keep moving, we need to find help,"* and pointed forward. Her eyes were wide and terrified, but she understood enough to keep moving.

In the tall grass we found another lady, older and just as naked and exposed as us. She was terribly old, time had ravaged her. She was sobbing but at least she spoke English. She asked over and over, *was she in bed?* I think she suffered from dementia as nothing I said or did resonated with her. The other lady and I took her by each arm and continued walking through the tall grass, looking for a road or farmhouse or anything that could help.

You probably think this is a dream. No, this was very real. The situations and locations were the same as the dreams, but this was intensely different. Vivid. I can close my eyes now and hear the wind through the grass, I can hear the laboured breathing of the old lady as we made our way through the night, bathed under the red glow of the sky and an unseen light source. I can't explain how it is real, I just know that it was.

I don't know how long we were walking but we discovered others. We found and huddled with a blind German woman and I found a little girl no more than five or six whom I carried. Eventually there were dozens of us, walking, silently, herd-like, towards a deep red glow on the horizon. There seemed to be no end in sight, just an unbearably infinite field of long grass. I was tired, aching from the cold and from carrying the child. I felt like I could just crash down, bury my face in the soil and sleep, but still we walked, a train of raw and exposed women walking towards a limitless horizon.

There were maybe a dozen or so women in front of us. I do not know their names or remember their faces, but they began chattering, then chattering became shouts and shouts became screams. They started panicking, running in circles, splintering off from each other, and then one by one they were sucked into the sky, rising and spinning. Their screams disappearing into silence.

My group had stopped. Beneath my toes I could feel the soil begin to tremble and I felt a wind on my face. The African lady began shouting while the old woman continually asked, *"Is it breakfast? Is it breakfast?"*

The child, heavy in my arms, hung on tightly and began sobbing, and I can still remember how her tears felt against my skin. Suddenly there was a whoosh and we all began to scream, and as we screamed, we began to lift off the ground, ascending into the night, swirling. I held on to the girl. The old lady flashed past me, her face laughing as we shot up into the sky. There was an intense red light and pain, such excruciating pain, screaming, maybe mine, maybe someone else's. I felt the girl fall from me, her small hands had been grabbing at me, grasping for me. That pain filled every fibre of my body and then blackness… and then silence.

I came to, and I was stood in a line of women in the gloom of a large room. There were red lights set in the floor beneath. I looked behind me and could not see the black woman, the child or the senile lady. Behind me was a woman, naked like I, with her head down, hair matted to her face, holding herself. I tried to ask her where we were, but I couldn't find the words to speak. I could see that her mouth was taped up with a skin-coloured plastic. I tried to pull at mine but could not find an overlap to tug at. It was as if it had been inserted into my face and not on top of it. I felt no pain where it had been inserted, just a strange numbness.

I couldn't hear anything other than the rushing of air in my ears and a pressure, the same sensation as when a plane is taking off. It was not cold where we were but clammy and warm. We were so close together all of us were practically touching each other, pushed against each other. I didn't know if I had been drugged, kidnapped or was trapped in some cult or military experiment. I began to panic, I began to feel claustrophobic. I knew where I was, it was all making sense.

It was as if I had been placed under some sort of spell where certain parts of my brain were functioning, but other parts had been switched off to the reality of what was really happening. Why would I walk in a field full of nude women? It was all part of the illusion these things created, and now I believed I was in their actual environment, behind the curtain so to speak. This wasn't my street, my flat or a field; this was where they took me, took others like me.

From in front, over what must have been a line of dozens of women all single file slowly walking forward, was a bright red light. The red light was moving towards me and over the line of women. As it got closer, I could see that it was an object. A bright red light with two enormous metal wings either side. I thought it had to be the owl, the owl in its true form. The women in front started to panic and covered their heads as the winged light flew over us dispersing a spray. I felt the droplets go all over my hair, on to my shoulders, some of it on to my face and suddenly I began to feel calm, almost content. The owl light disappeared out of view over what I could only imagine was dozens, if not more, women like me.

Was I on board a spacecraft or a hidden alien base? I do believe I was. Especially after what I was about to see.

We slowly walked forward. I had no control over this, just the instinct to keep walking as I had in the field. Some of the women up front were trying desperately to turn around, one

even managing to climb on top of another only for the owl light
to swoop down and push her back into the line. We had no choice
but to keep moving forward. It was reminiscent of scenes from
the Second World War, of Auschwitz.

We, it seemed, were being separated into different lines. As
I walked forward, I saw we had entered a huge expanse, like a
cavern. There were hundreds, maybe thousands of women in
here, all being herded through sections. Older ladies in one line,
children in another; all sorts of different women in different
lines. There was a brighter light, whiter light in here, somewhere
in the middle; the roof of the place was incredibly high up, like a
cathedral, with red lights intermittent in lines, in rows from the
roof to the ground.

The floor in this area seemed to be like walking barefoot on
seaweed. It was organic and wet, slippery; it looked to be a deep
shade of red but with the lights it was difficult to say. I think
now they could have been human remains; I'm not sure, maybe
it was an organic substance they grew or was used on the craft.
Maybe it was growing from the remains from us. Maybe it was
a fertilizer or a compost. I just looked at it with a contented
understanding that all of this was perfectly natural, as if I had
been sedated.

It was humid in there, stuffy, and I could only breathe
through my nose and the smell was awful, sweat, sick, pee and
shit, just an awful smell of illness and death, fear and people
stripped down to their basic functions. I burn incense every
day, constantly, as that awful smell still lingers in my nose and I
attempt to drown it out, smell something less vile and revolting.
Imagine a thousand scared, naked people, women, all stuffed
into a hangar, going to the toilet while they are shuffling along,
tightly packed, chest to back.

The owl lights were floating around us, some hovering,
some flying in a straight line, like they were monitoring us,
shepherding us ever forward. I saw an old woman topple over

in a line next to us. The knees of the woman behind hitting her in the back of the head and neck. An owl light swept over us and hovered, and from the light, the eye area, a long thing, pipe or tube, six feet or more, extended out until it was over her head. It must have attached itself to her. I couldn't see her through all the limbs in the way, but it flew off without strain with the lady attached by the head, and flew high up and then away from us. That was someone's mother, someone's grandmother, just taken away to what end I do not know but no doubt horrific on every single level imaginable. I want you to imagine your mother or grandmother or your daughter experiencing this. There is nothing like this on Earth. It's sickening, it's horrific. We are people, not animals.

There is a break in the session as Susan was struggling emotionally and physically. It was a traumatic experience. Her eyes had been closed as she saw herself back in the environment, describing every detail, answering every question I asked. It was my duty of care to stop the session until she found herself, once again, capable of carrying on.

An hour later Susan asked me to continue, asking I not miss a word out, to ensure every word was recorded. This next part of the session is extremely harrowing and disturbing. Due caution is advised.

Susan: It was as if we were being herded into areas based on our type, body type, age, health. We moved along, squashed up against each other, and we left the cavern and down a small tunnel, barely tall enough to walk through. Hunched I shuffled through. Up ahead I could hear agony, crying, screaming, recognizable sounds but muffled; it seemed that everything up here was muffled, the air, the sounds of the place, all muffled. I could feel the air rushing in my ears.

As we walked forward, I could hear women up front gasping,

retching, talking, shouting, screaming, pleading. I found that my mouthpiece, the plastic bit, had vanished. I can't recall it being taken out or falling out; my mouth tasted like I had been trying to inhale the smoke of burning plastic or rubber. I took a huge gulp of clammy sweaty air and thought I would be sick. I felt something wet and chunky hit my back and I can only guess that the woman behind me had been sick on to me. There was no room, nowhere to move, only forward, little shuffling baby steps, one at a time. We were walking through bodily waste.

We emerged into a larger room, brighter. The walls had some form of organic substance growing on them, almost like a mincemeat. I can't explain what it was, only what it looked like: it was like little tubes of solid meat, tiny tubes. There was more room to move and some women stepped out of the column, some fell, some crouched down, some stretched, everyone looked terrified but too subdued to do anything about it. I looked for an exit, somewhere to hide, but I couldn't even begin to comprehend where I was. It was as if my basic instinct of fight or flight had been turned off.

A substance sprayed upon me; I can't say where it came from, it was warm and bitty. Some of the women were crying trying to rub it off. We were all huddled in the room and I would estimate there were over a hundred of us. I can still remember some of their faces to this day. Terrified faces. The smell stale and sickening. Some women were huddled together, one lay on the floor sobbing, one I think had fainted. She was taken away by an owl light. In my mind I thought, I've been here before, it's just now I'm remembering, they will do their thing and I'll be set free. I just have to keep my wits about me, play along, maybe they had forgotten to neutralise me, maybe that came at the end and all of this would just become another dream.

Soon we instinctively began walking again and we continued into… it is something so cruel, so horrific, I can't. It can only be likened to an abattoir. A factory of some description. It's not fair this happened, it's not fair to me, to any of us, and people don't want to know. They want to fucking laugh and call me a liar and a fraud, and guess what, probably someone you know has or will go through this and because of the idiots, the bullies. Victims of this atrocity are living a life of fear, alone and frightened. People like us are ridiculed in the press and on TV. This was a fucking abattoir; do you understand me? Women, girls of all ages are being subjected to something inhumane and no one, no one is helping us.

My herd, my line, we had it easy, we took it in turns to have a pipe go into our genitals and a needle in the neck, that's what we had, and we were the lucky ones. It felt like a smear but with a suction attached. They were taking something small from us, small enough but on a mass scale it would be enough for whatever they needed. I stood in line while tendrils, pipes, tubes came from out of the wall, feeling us, inserting into us, pricking us with a needle or barb in the back of the head. It was sharp intense pains. I felt like something was being scraped and sucked out from inside me.

It was the other things I saw that terrify me because once I am done providing whatever it is they take from women like me, as we get older, they take something else, then they take more, then they use you for other things and one day you are not waking up, never going home and you are just a piece of all of this waiting, praying for death, but they fill you with tubes and needles and keep you alive.

I was sick until I couldn't be sick anymore when I witnessed what looked like half-men, the bottom half of men, from the waist down. Everything below intact and just a cluster of pipes and wires, tendrils for a torso, for the rest of the body, attached to an overhead pipe or something. I have no idea what had become of the rest of the bodies. These legs were moving, their penis erect and a series of women, on conveyer belts, shackled down by an organic mass, like coral, something so strange, were presented to the lower halves of the men. The women were presented face down with their bottoms up and the men, whatever you call them, were having some weird mechanical jerky sex with them. Once they were done another woman would be presented. There were about fifty of these mating things. They looked like they had been men. I can't tell you much more. I can only speculate that it was some type of insemination procedure. I don't know, I'm trying to tell you in ways that I can explain. So much is so insane and brutal that finding the words, even after all this time, is hard.

I saw pregnant women being milked like cows. Tendrils like tubes stuck into their breasts as the women gave pitiful exhausted moans. The milk filling up transparent cocoon or egg-like objects. Every part of us from birth till death was being utilized.

I saw in one section below us a whole area of women giving birth, lying on the mince-like substance on the floor. No one helping. They lay there screaming and panting. The still-pregnant mothers huddled against the wall, hands covering their heads, their ears, facing the wall, trying to remain invisible, trying to wake up from the nightmare. The women giving birth were not assisted, just pushing and screaming on the filthy floor, dozens of them. One of them pushed out a child with a huge grunt. Afterbirth spilled on to the floor, the mother grappled with what little strength she had to get her baby up to her chest, but a light owl swooped in and the baby was gone, umbilical cord ripped as it left. The woman lay there screaming, begging as one of the bulbous creatures, the sort I had seen on Mog, on Aunty, walked on its tall, impossibly thin legs towards her and dropped unceremoniously on to her. Her pain, her shouts muffled as the bloated creature covered her, its legs, its tendrils filling every orifice until she lay still. I could see half a dozen women lying still with bulbous colourful sacks either eating them or planting in them, I don't know.

Once we had our injections, we continued along what must have been an upper tier; below we could see other tiers. There were thousands of women. In the section beneath us, past the birthing area, were dozens of babies, sat naked in a circle, like an arena. The faceless black men, with the thin arms and legs, stood, watching the babies. Light owls seemed to take away the quietest babies, the babies exhibiting little fight for life, while the crying ones lay there being admired, sold off, who knows for what purpose with the alien beings I had first seen at Sian's. I had always thought they were the ones in control, the top of the hierarchy. The overseers.

Past that was an area where the bulbous sack creatures were squashed into a large area; they looked like bloated bioluminescent pigs from above. I thought, was this a herding area? Maybe even where they bred these disgusting animals, but I saw as we shuffled past that they were feeding on children, babies, maybe the sickly ones, the dying ones. I hope whatever they were doing was painless and quick but deep down I knew they were consuming, extracting every essence, every nutrient. These images cannot be wiped from one's mind; they haunt you forever. Did I want to jump off and fight them? Do you think I could have got there and saved all those children and babies, hundreds of them? Then what, Gavin? Get all action hero and fly the ship back to Earth, save the day and get a medal? I could barely move, don't you get it. I could barely string two thoughts together. If I could have saved them, I would have. If I could have blown the whole place up and killed everyone, I would have because that's a more decent, more humane death than these things will ever give you. It's a horrendous death camp up there; women, children and babies are dying, being harvested up there and no one down here cares.

Women are complaining of irregular period pains, stomach cramps, pains behind their eyes, sickness, diarrhoea, strange dreams and visions, inexplicable paranoia, fear of certain roads, certain places, times of night, times of day, they think they see ghosts and shadows before they sleep, when they wake up in the night, but all of it, all of it is them, these aliens. They treat us like livestock. They are extracting and harvesting body parts, hormones, blood, bodily fluids, our lives, all of us and I don't know what it's for. Is it to eat us, for medicine? Are these the intergalactic herbal remedy store people and are we the berries and herbs that make them think they are living a healthy lifestyle? I don't know.

Yes, I saw more; is this enough for you yet?

I saw a conveyor belt or some sort and on it was body parts, dismembered limbs, the corpses of the very old, the very young, those who didn't have the fortitude to survive their ordeal.

But it was the area that the conveyor belt passed that made me the most terrified. Below in an arena, that's the best way I can describe it, an arena where hundreds and hundreds of women were herded. Their screams, their voices, pleading, crying, begging will haunt me forever. The women, the ones I could see, seemed to be older, past forty, maybe fifty, maybe their childbearing days were over, I can't say for sure. Some were dragged off by the light owls, maybe they still had a use that needed them alive. The others though desperately tried to get anyway from a hub, climbing on top of each other, punching, fighting, no dignity, away from a central hub where a great many tendrils, pipes, whatever we are to call them were grabbing random women and conducting a quick medical procedure. A check-up, a medical procedure as tendrils probed their cavities, examined, needles sticking, tubes sucking. Always checking were they still good, were they still in date, were they worth anything, could a profit be made on them. Some were harvested, right there and then. Pipes filled them, they were pulled apart; pipes and tubes sucking up every drop and a sack of skin and bones deposited on the conveyor belt. Dozens of women in an instant gone, dismembered. Their life, their memories, the world they had created, nothing more than a mineral or a liquid for some alien industrialists or farmers.

The lucky ones – they weren't totally extracted, they were pushed down a hole, but where they went, I could not see.

By telling you this, I can't go missing. I can't go up on the craft and never be seen again as now if I go missing everyone will know what's happened and someone will have to help me, help the others. These things can't be as brazen as to keep coming for me. We must stop this. If I get pregnant on that ship I am never coming back. Myself and my baby would be harvested and I will just be another statistic; another missing person, another loony gone.

On the ship, my group were huddled into a new room, a wall thick with the organic substance, a dome, red lights in the ceiling. Women were screaming, panicking, they had just seen what had happened below. We all looked at the walls waiting for tubes and tendrils to shoot out to start harvesting us but instead a mist rose into the room and soon it was as if we were all in a shower; calming warming steam and the relaxing droplets covered me.

I remember nothing more from on board the ship.

I woke up. I was in a field. I was lying naked on the ground. I was surrounded in a familiar red light. I thought, when will ever end? I stood up and there in front of me, just a few feet, was the red brake lights of my car. My clothes were bundled by the car door. The car was about twenty feet up a track in a field, and had stopped just on an entrance to some woodland. I can't remember driving up there. I put on my clothes and sat in the car. The time said 20.03. It had been three minutes. I had witnessed a living hell, a scene from Hades, a nightmare that seemed to last for hours upon hours, and it had all happened in three minutes.

I was terribly thirsty. I had come on and I had a vicious pain behind my right eye. They had let me go... for now.

Eulogy

And death shall have no dominion.
Dead man naked they shall be one
With the man in the wind and the west moon;
When their bones are picked clean and the clean bones gone,
They shall have stars at elbow and foot;
Though they go mad they shall be sane,
Though they sink through the sea they shall rise again;
Though lovers be lost love shall not;
And death shall have no dominion.
Dylan Thomas, "And Death Shall Have No Dominion"

It had been a strenuous session. Susan sat there staring at her collection of pictures that depicted the horrors on board what I could only assume was a spacecraft of gigantic proportions. I had stared intently at the sickeningly horrific images of women herded past nightmarish inventions of torture, extraction and industry as she narrated her equally nightmarish vision of a mechanical hell. As curious as I had been, I could not stomach the illustrations of horror for long and had to look away. I had read of alien abduction, experiments, inter-species mating and cattle mutilation for decades, this was not something new, but this was something more – this was genocide.

Susan had taken great care and detail to ensure that each picture was as accurate as she could remember. If she was not dreaming it, if this were all true, then savage acts of depravity were being conducted on defenceless women and children from all over the planet on a huge scale. My revulsion, my repugnance turned to anger – surely hundreds, if not thousands of women in this world do not simply go missing without someone in power knowing? Had this been happening since time immemorial?

I had little to say to Susan; I was numb, it was late, after 2am. I asked for her leave. I felt guilty for leaving but I had to go. I needed to process the words, the images from the book. I asked when I could come back. She thought we were finished, that was it; I had all my pieces to begin to put the puzzle together, but so much did not make sense. There were connections I had not made, theories I had not yet thought through. Despite having so much, I needed to come back to it with a fresher mind. Where did they get the males that procreated with the women on board the ship? Why harvest old ladies if they were no longer of use? Where had they been taken? Based on the description Susan had given me I imagined a great hulking industrial complex sat out there in the cold of space. Our world a defenceless ball of blue light, like a beacon, as the visitors came and went selecting the meat, rounding us up, harvesting and culling.

She said I had enough to warn the world. She made me promise that no matter whatever happened I must publish the book. She handed me the publishing agreements, disclaimer and terms of agreement form signed and dated. She made me promise that I would not contact mental health support, her parents or any medical professional on her behalf unless she inflicted any harm on herself or others. I was bound to this, though I begged her to seek medical advice. It couldn't hurt to get help.

I asked, had they come back? Would they come back for her? She answered me with stone-cold silence. Was she insane? I do not know but whatever she believed had happened had terrified her. I left that night shocked by the imagery, aghast at her words. I was sick into a doorway not far from her flat. It had been too much. My mind whirled. Was this a horrific fantasy? How could someone create something so detailed, so macabre?

Susan and I had agreed a few weeks were needed for me to piece together all the information that I had collated. There were reams of notes, questions upon questions, and whole days' worth of recordings.

As I sifted through them I grew fearful of the night sky and what may have been peering down from the invisible heavens. Worryingly, I wondered if she was planning to disappear.

Several weeks later I was able to continue the final sessions, consisting of further inquiries I had formulated after processing her testimonial.

Susan was relieved to see me and had a pot of tea ready. She had made a great many cigarettes for these final sessions. Inside I felt melancholic. I had grown fond of her. I wanted to see her unshackled from this lifestyle, to get to a point where she could move on and smile, be unafraid of the night. I wanted to see her flourish and blossom, to regain her educational and vocational goals, to find new friends, reattach herself back to her family and find what so many of us want – to love and be loved.

I explained to Susan that I just wanted her to talk freely, to hypothesise, to go on her instinct. I have included my questions; please understand that her answers are just her own observations and thoughts.

Final sessions merged to form closing testimony

G.L. Davies (GLD): Please don't think of my questions as impertinent. I'm simply looking for clarification on what you believe has happened to you. I have had time to reread and re-evaluate your account and I know from my experience a great many questions will be asked by readers and investigators, so to put it simply we are filling the holes, connecting the dots so to speak. So, Susan, I would like to ask you. Who are these beings? What do you believe them to be?

Susan: As you have seen I have conducted a great deal of research into alien sightings, UFOs, alien abductions, cattle mutilations, you name it. If it is part of Ufology I have read, watched or listened to it. No matter how far-fetched it might seem, I have taken it apart, as deep inside there could be a sliver of fact.

I had no interest in this before the events began. Though I did enjoy science fiction, I was not a fan of *Star Trek* or *Doctor Who* but more classic films like *Solaris*.

Did I tell you that I've examined every aspect of mental health to determine if I am in fact clinically insane? If there is anything capable of creating such a large deep psychological episode I have studied it. Did you know there are those who suffer from a very rare mental disorder called Boanthropy where people believe they are cows, often going as far as to behave as such. *(People have been found in fields with cows, walking on all fours and chewing grass as if they were a true member of the herd. Those with Boanthropy do not seem to realise what they're doing when they act like a cow, leading researchers to believe that this odd mental disorder is brought on by dreams or even hypnotism. Interestingly, it is believed that Boanthropy is even referred to in the Bible, as King Nebuchadnezzar is described as being "driven from men and did eat grass as oxen".)*

Look, I know that someone who's mentally ill is the last person to know it. That's a definition of mental illness. I wish I was ill. That would be simple. But I know I'm not. You'll just have to believe me or not. I believe this is real, these beings are real.

I believe that these beings are very old and advanced, on a technological level that far exceeds anything we have a grasp of. I have read theories regarding humans from the future coming back for genetic samples and the like, but these things – I don't believe they are our future selves. I don't subscribe to the theory of a hollow earth with these creatures emerging from the ground and taking us away, or to the dark side of the moon. This hell, their hell, is beyond, way beyond that. I believe they found us in our infancy and have permitted us to thrive and cover the world, harvesting us a little to begin with and increasingly as the population grew. We are not a threat to them, we are defenceless. For all our scientific marvels, we haven't explored much of space, and even if we did and settled on other planets it would just provide them with more sources for them to harvest.

GLD: So, you don't believe that they seeded us here on Earth deliberately?

Susan: If they had, I think they would live in plain sight. They would have huge factories and processing plants on the planet. They would simply breed us like cattle, in our millions. I think they stumbled upon us in our early days, making themselves known to early man and then hid. I read an interesting theory that the harvester, the processing craft, may just be one of many, of different kinds, in our galaxy, taking what they need at any one time. You must remember that these things are hugely advanced – they can control and manipulate time, space, our minds, our technology. Maybe they live in a dimension slightly different to ours, and can move across. If they wanted to reap a huge harvest in one go, they could, at any point in man's climb to civilization. I really believe that.

It is possible that of the seven or eight billion people on the planet that only a small percentage of us have what they need so they need to process the extraction in smaller numbers in different ways. There is no need for a great big operation where the entire world witnesses their arrival and then panics. Maybe we're a little bit more problematic for them now. We have nuclear weapons and bad tempers, and perhaps it is best for the beings to hide out of the way, though I'm not sure if we could inflict any damage on them. I can't offer much more than that.

GLD: Do you think there was a hierarchy amongst the

various beings you saw?

Susan: Definitely! I believe the skinny faceless men are like the overseers. I think they may be the scientists amongst the operation, choosing and sampling us, seeing which of us have what is needed for extraction.

When I watched them studying the babies on board the spacecraft it was as if they were selecting which ones could stay for further study, whatever they do. It makes me feel ill thinking that the male babies may end up as the mating machines. They were clearly half-human, grotesque. These beings have no regard for life at all.

The red lights, or owl lights – I think of them as the shepherds. They probably have some form of artificial intelligence that keeps an eye on us, keeps us moving in the right direction. The bulbous insect-like jellyfish seemed to be part of the extraction process. I have no idea if they were advanced or not, maybe like a pet, a farmyard animal, I don't know. I've never encountered anything like them in my research, but something similar was said to be like a hive mind that would feed on the nutrients found in us.

The red woman with the flowing robes – I have no idea what she was. Her appearance was the most consistent with other reports of alien beings. It had the large eyes and some sort of breathing apparatus. Maybe it was a hybrid, half-human, half-alien. I can't be sure. Anything I suggest can't be proven anyway. Maybe someone out there who has had a similar experience can offer something more substantial on the red woman's relationship to the skinny faceless men and owl lights. Maybe she makes the decision on whom is to be selected, maybe she is the herald of the horrors that are to come. Just pray you don't see her, or any of these things for that matter.

We can't understand the actions of these beings when they are altogether inhuman, and possibly thousands if not hundreds of thousands of years more advanced than us. We are just like chimps or animals to them. I can't even begin to explain how their technology works. It is beyond our understanding. We are nowhere close.

GLD: They are very brazen, if people are being taken from their homes and beds, some from cars, some from built-up areas; some people come back with injury or illness, and some don't come back at all. You claim to have seen hundreds if not thousands of women on board the craft. Why are they so open about it?

Susan: If you think how big the world is, and how many people there are out there then how easy would it be to take scattered individuals? Let's just say, for instance, you took a couple of dozen from the United States every month, a handful from the UK, from the other European countries, that's a small fraction of the number of people who go missing. Half a million people under 21 go missing in the USA every year. Then there are all the other countries – you could soon get up to thousands. Most of these I believe are put back, perhaps with bad dreams and illness, but it's put down to just that. Others, they keep. It's like any business or industry for them, but instead of chickens or cows or potatoes or corn they are utilizing people.

This is not a new theory I made up; the idea of being harvested by alien beings has been around for millennia. We recorded sacrifices and human offerings to the gods in the sky from the time we started to paint in the caves. It's terrifying. Next time people are eying up some meat in the supermarket, think about how the animal was killed, and how would you feel if that was your children, your mother? Not so humane is it now? There are 1.5 billion cows in the world, bred to be eaten, to be worn, to provide milk, and that's how the aliens use us. I ate meat like everyone else before this, and to be honest I didn't much mind where my burger or fish came from. But seeing what I did, it's put me off, disgusted me for life. If we treat animals that way, then why should the aliens care much for us? Because we can talk or pray? That doesn't matter. If you know what I know, you may take a frightened moment to think, *"Oh my god I'm being treated like an animal, I wish we had treated our animals better."*

One day you may wake up ill, confused from a terrible dream, stomach pains, cramps, pains behind your eyes, pains in your neck, pains in your groin, in your anus and every time you close your eyes you know deep down you have been somewhere, seen something and none of it will make any sense. Guess what? You have been selected, it's your turn, you just won the fucking lottery.

This isn't some pious rant about the environment and overpopulation. No, I didn't care and the only reason I care now is that I have seen mothers, grandmothers, little girls treated like cattle, slaughtered like cattle, impregnated like animals, dissected like beasts and left to rot cold and alone in some far-off space factory. There is no God up there for us, no mercy, no negotiation, no fighting back. There is pain, there is suffering, there is fear and there is doom.

GLD: Do you think our governments know what is happening? If not our government, then the military, scientists, astronauts, anyone?

Susan: There is a lot of speculation that our governments have crashed alien technology, made deals with advanced alien races, but I don't know. Wouldn't it be more obvious somehow? But I think these harvesters will come and go regardless of what we know or don't know, say or do.

Just because I am here talking to you right now does not mean I am safe and out of harm's way. I have got off lightly so far and as I get older they will take more from me, until there is nothing left to take, and I am just another crazy missing person.

If I go missing tomorrow, Gavin, vanish off the face of the Earth, what will you think? Will you think I am dead? Maybe I killed myself? Or went hiking, some crazy, friendless girl who sadly never came back? There are so many women of all ages living alone, it's easier than having lovers, partners, family, and one day they go missing and the thing is – no one really noticed them there to begin with, and so no one cares when they vanish.

Apart from a few people I work with, how many in Haverfordwest know I even exist? No one in this street knows who I am. No one in this block of flats knows my name. They probably think you're my fancy man if they see you; you're the only person who visits. Maybe they think I'm a prostitute and you pay me for sex. Or that you're my pimp or drug dealer. No one cares about a stranger's life, and when they do, they assume the worse. When I move out of here, do you think there will be a leaving party, gifts and a fond farewell. No, Gavin, I will leave and within less than a week I will be forgotten. No one will remember me other than my closest family.

GLD: And me, you can't forget you have let me into your life, and I do care. I want this to stop so you can have the life you deserve.

Susan: How do we stop it?

GLD: There has to be a way. What are your reasons for asking to me to publish this?

Susan: It sounds hackneyed to say I want to raise awareness, like I'm asking for donations for a charity. If one person reads this and realises it is happening to them maybe they will keep the message growing, until there are scores of us, an army of us, until our governments and scientists realise we are under attack, know that innocent defenceless women are being slaughtered and tortured. Someone must take notice, someone must help, to try and stop it.

I want my life to have meaning, not just a nameless woman

lost in the void to a faceless aggressor. Maybe one day, long from now, this book will make sense, will be believed by millions. Maybe we can't stop what's coming but maybe we can change our lives for the better, live every moment as if it's our last.

GLD: But what if the governments are aware of what is happening, what if there is a deal? Even if the governments do believe you, want to protect you, you said yourself that these beings have advanced and sophisticated grasps of time, space, our minds, technology, incredible things. What if we are not able to defend you, help you, protect women and people like you? What happens then?

Susan: Then, Gavin, this is the eulogy of one lonely woman.

GLD: Why don't you take all of this, all the pictures, your testimonial to the press, I'll come with you? Surely the fear of being outed and ridiculed far outweighs the negatives of what could happen? Maybe someone somewhere would bring you in for constant surveillance, monitoring. It's not the best way of living but it's better than the alternative?

Susan: To the press? So I can be an exclusive on a front page? Maybe I could be the star of a big brother reality show where people place bets on when they will abduct me? What do I tell my parents, when I'm plastered all over the front page of every newspaper written for a five-year-old? Haven't you listened to anything I've said? I would rather take my own life than let my parents know what is happening to me. I would rather die mutilated and cut up like beef than bring the shame of this upon my parents, my family. At least now they just think I am just some bipolar druggy dropout or whatever they think I am.

Look, there's no one out there who can help me, who will believe me. Unless you've experienced the same you can't fathom what this is all about. This is about planting seeds now so more and more people start to think about all this, start to take it seriously.

This is not pride. Revealing myself is not going to change one damn thing, but the message will. I will go missing and die, or I will simply die at my own hand. I am alone and that is why I need this account published so people like me no longer have to die in silence. This way people will start to believe there is something happening, and maybe one day enough people will be talking about this seriously and not in a tabloid way. One day someone serious, someone qualified will ask why are so many women going missing? Why are so many healthy women getting clean bills of health one day and a few weeks later are riddled with cancer?

Adding my name to the book will only draw negative attention. An anonymous woman could be any girl in any street, in any town in the world. It has more power that way. The message is the fight, the power. Nobody wants this to happen to their daughter or sister or mother.

GLD: What if you are not suffering alone? You mentioned during the sessions that you thought you saw your mother, grandmother and aunty in the fields walking towards the light. Is it possible they are interested in whole bloodlines? Your mother, however, was obviously not from that bloodline and it would seem that she inadvertently married into a family that was under the insidious design of otherworldly visitors and may have inherited this curse. What if your mother does know and a woman of her constitution could at least help you both make sense of this, speak to professionals, find the right way to face this, to raise the awareness you need?

Susan: I often wondered if this was more than just me. I had the dream where my family were involved. Maybe certain bloodlines have an attractive quality of blood, genetic material make-up, who knows? My grandmother and aunty both died terrible deaths caused by cancer and Mother has always been distant and aloof. Maybe that is the case, but she never mentioned it, will never mention it and neither can I. Her profession comes first. If there was ever a hint I was talking about UFOs and aliens, then the pain I would cause her would be greater than anything I could ever physically do to her.

You really must understand, I don't have that support from friends and family to talk about this. You are the closest I have ever come to dealing with this. I can never ever let my family know. This is about the message.

Sometimes I'll read a UFO report or see something on TV or in the papers of some poor woman talking about this and they get a few columns and a lot of mockery. Jokes about anal probes and little green men. It's all a big joke, sensationalised garbage to the media and they thrive on it, and I hope, just pray in ten years, a hundred years, someone, somewhere reads this account and knows it to be real and starts to change the world's opinion on the subject. How many times can I hammer the word *message*?

So many people already know the truth, but they can't come forward for fear of ridicule and being labelled as a crank, a fantasist. I don't think it's an organized cover-up, but simply small-minded people afraid of what they cannot control. Each generation believing what the one before them told them and accepting it as absolute truth.

We have done this to ourselves, and as soon as you say no, this is wrong, there are terrible things happening in this world, then you get stuck with a great big label of being mentally ill and as a fantasist. How many people are suffering, how many are afraid and there is no one for them to go to?

My mother is part of the problem. She's a cog in the ever-turning machine telling us what is right to believe and what is wrong. I pray that soon there is an event that shows the world that they were here all the time. It's been ignored for too long.

GLD: What if then this book catches fire, and people start reading it, talking about it and your parents read all of this and realise it's you, it's been you all along, their little girl at the centre of this extraterrestrial nightmare?

Susan: I will simply deny it. But Mother would never in a million years read this, or associate me with it. She does not have the capacity for such imagination.

GLD: You saw something on the estuary with Adrian. You described it as a giant ball of flame. I wonder why they are so open in showing themselves on the estuary? Any ideas? Would you say there was an obvious connection between the ball of light and the events that transpired?

Susan: I always believed the two were connected, part of the same infiltration. I don't know why people see these lights so often on the estuary. I have researched sightings in the area going back fifty years.

One possibility, and it's literally just an idea and I have nothing to support this, something on the estuary is making them visible. Maybe it's the chemicals in the air or toxins, I'm not sure.

Something that sprang to mind just now could be, what if the estuary is like an airport for them, a landing zone. A rift in which they enter from their world into ours. Maybe it's all the water in the area, maybe the industry, something they use to navigate into the area. There are lots of UFO reports around fjords and waterways. Maybe they use the water for energy, and as they approach, they are visible for a small amount of time until they power back into some sort of cloaking technology. Very science fiction I know.

No one can deny the number of unusual phenomena on the waterway. There have been so many sightings of fiery orbs and lights. Ghost hunters need to stop wasting their times in graveyards and start staking out the estuary, there is so much happening down there.

GLD: Maybe something like the Hessdalen lights? *(The Hessdalen lights are unexplained lights observed in a 7.5-mile-long* *stretch of the Hessdalen valley in rural central Norway. They appear both by day and by night, and seem to float through and above the valley. They are usually bright white, yellow, or red, and can appear above and below the horizon. Duration of the phenomenon may be a few seconds to well over an hour. Sometimes the lights move with enormous speed; at other times they seem to sway slowly back and forth. On yet other occasions, they hover in mid-air. Unusual lights have been reported in the region since at least the 1930s. Especially high activity occurred between December 1981 and mid-1984, in which period the lights were being observed 15–20 times per week, attracting many overnight tourists who arrived in for a sighting. As of 2010, the number of observations has dwindled, with only ten to 20 sightings made yearly.)*

Susan: Exactly, even though the lights remain a mystery, at least they are being studied and accepted as a phenomenon. Our lights on the estuary are sighted regularly, even reported to the police, the port authority and the press, and no one seems any closer to understanding their nature. I am not aware of any serious study into the lights on the Milford Haven estuary. More people need to pay attention down there.

To answer your question though, I do believe they are connected to the experiences I have suffered and encountered. Too many coincidences for them not to be.

GLD: The visitors showed you some very violent pictures of a harrowing calamity in Pembrokeshire. Many people reading this right now are going to be concerned that a disaster is imminent. Why do you think the visitors showed you this? Should we heed it as a warning?

Susan: I think the beings were using us for study. They showed me awful, terrible things to create a response. Maybe it was to subjugate me into feeling hopeless, frightened. It certainly worked. They took me on a roller coaster of emotions and feelings, and from that I imagine they saw me as suitable for harvesting.

Regarding the disaster, I could not tell you if it will happen or not. I was given a front row seat to what looked like the end of the world. It was awful, the scale of destruction was unlike anything I could ever imagine. It was like a nuclear holocaust. People were smashed, ripped and burned, and all of it seemed to centre on the estuary. I saw Haverfordwest in ruins and tens of thousands of people live in and around that area.

It is always going to be difficult in deciphering what the aliens' intentions are. Was it part of a process to produce more chemicals from me, maybe witnessing that utter, mind-blowing scale of destruction sweetens the meat. Perhaps it produces a satisfying hormonal or chemical reaction. Maybe they were showing me what will happen as they are telling me to mentally cease resisting as everything I think matters is pointless anyway. I will die.

We will all die.

I often wonder if that vision of impending destruction was just Pembrokeshire, maybe it was the world. Maybe we are all doomed to die or live in the ashes of a super-disaster.

Can I reassure anyone that it's not going to happen? No. I have no idea and every day I wait to hear the ground rumble and tremble, and the sky to be filled with smoke and flame, and think *oh dear it is happening*. I have kept away from that area since the encounters. I have seen the destruction and I have no interest into witnessing it again.

GLD: Why a fox and an owl? Why is the imagery of these animals so significant?

Susan: I think they are part of the drugs or chemicals they use to neutralise us. It may not even be intentional, maybe everyone sees and has different experiences, but the owl is the most common earth-based creature associated with alien abduction.

The fox was always relatable, always seemed to be familiar. Maybe the fox represents me, us, people. We are never safe.

The fox lives a life in constant fear of hunters, poison, farmers, traps and guns. Beautiful creatures just trying to survive. The fox does not wake up with the intention of causing havoc and damaging profits. The fox looks for the easiest point between A and B to survive, to eat. What do you think a fox would rather hunt and kill, a chicken or go up against a pit bull?

The fox just wants to sleep safely amongst its cubs, with its belly full. But they are seen as outlaws and pests of the countryside. How many mothers, human mothers, simply want the same as a fox? They want happy children asleep safe at night with a full belly and everything they need in life. We are not that different from animals when you strip us down to our basic needs. That's not putting the human race down; just shows deep down we are just trying to survive through each day.

I just wanted a life, to survive, to have a good life, to strive, to accomplish my goals, but the aliens see me as a commodity, a pest, ready to be exploited and harvested.

The owl is them. It represents a superior intellect, a powerful predator watching us as we sleep, silently descending upon us with no warning, no defence. I'm not saying owls are aliens. I'm saying the owl represents the behaviour and motives of the alien beings. Our brains formulate imagery and themes to help us make sense of trauma and what is going on around us. It is commonly known in psychology that we do this.

GLD: How long has it been since they last made themselves known to you?

Susan: It has been at least three years since I have been directly aware of them. I still suffer from the vivid dreams and nightmares, if that is what they are. I still see the fox and the owl. They are still here, always watching. They are my shepherds.

GLD: What happens next, to you?

Susan: For the many months since we have spoken and

discussed this I wondered, what if? What if one day you knock upon my door and I'm not here to answer?

You helped me, Gavin. This was more than another paranormal book for you. I got the sense you cared, genuinely wanted to help.

You helped me realise that even when I am at my lowest, the days when I just want to die or become someone else, there are still beautiful things to be admired and treasured in this world.

I will never experience true love, true friendship again. I can't accept that into my life. I look at you, Gavin, and I wonder what effect our time together will have on you. Will you escape unscathed or will you start to see your own life decay? That is why I approached a man to document this, less dangerous than if it was a woman.

I hope you remain safe and find the answers you are looking for. You are a beacon of light for people like me, women who are fearful of the day's end, when sleep overwhelms, and we lose ourselves in the void of unconsciousness. Maybe you can herald a new era of acceptance, of change, a world where people are more prepared to help. Keep shining your light and shine it bright.

I still have my inheritance, which I was going to build a new life with, a career, but that's not going to be. I have been thinking if I am to be alone, it is better to be alone somewhere beautiful, somewhere incredible. If I am to be alone then let's paint on a smile and find a reason to live. I want to change the perception of generations. That's what I am fighting for.

I will travel, alone of course, see the world. The world will see just another backpacker, and should I go missing, then I am simply another statistic.

You have my last will and testament. Do not let my suffering be for nothing. Make people read this, make them see what is really happening in our world.

I feel so sad that I will never have what so many people take for granted. Those who you love, tell them that every day, make sure of it, because one day it could be you or them who is plucked like corn from the ground.

Interviews concluded July 2016

The documentation process continued for a further eighteen months; piecing together the testimonial, checking sources, investigating their credibility, and eventually I was able to present a suitable version to Susan.

I had remained in touch – more than a courtesy, I did not want something awful to happen to her. I checked in on her every week, using the excuse of a progress check or of a date or fact inquiry. I dreaded any delays in her response and a few times was tempted to knock on her flat door to make sure she was in good health. It is a tremendous responsibility to ensure someone you know does not fall prey to mental health issues, self-harm or worse. I would not count myself as a close friend of Susan, but at the very least I was a near neighbour concerned for her well-being.

She never hinted that there had been any return visits from the aliens. Did that mean it was over? They were going to leave her alone? Or had the catharsis of having her story recorded enabled her to free herself from her delusions? Which did I believe? I guess that's the question you're asking.

This is dangerous ground. It's easier to assume someone is mentally ill, rather than believing in aliens visiting the Earth.

I spent enough time with Susan to recognize that this was all real to her. The detail and intricacy of her account was of a different order to anything I have dealt with before or since. I'll come clean here – in the process of putting the weeks' worth of notes together I was pulled back into the experiences I recounted in *Haunted: Horror of Haverfordwest*. That's when I began to wonder – no, to worry – whether we really understood our world. Were there nefarious forces at work that inhabited unknown and unrecognized areas of reality? Could it be that demons, ghosts and spirits are in some sense "real"? And perhaps there were good ones as well. After all, most people in the world believe this, in some form, in gods and devils, angels and witches. Most Americans for instance believe in God the Father and Son, who descended to Earth and rose again to heaven, and in the spirit of the Holy Ghost. Many take the Bible literally, where demons and evil spirits, below the ground and above it, are legion. Look at any Sunday church congregation, with many overwhelmed by the life-changing presence of Spirit, and the people there have no doubt. Put the question to most scientists though, and they would say it's far more likely that there are alien life forms in the universe. It's indeed tough to believe that in a universe of this scale our planet is the only one harbouring life. If you take into account the possibilities and implications of quantum physics, with existence itself dependent on whether there's an observer to see it or not, with other universes almost necessary, parallel worlds branching out with every quantum event, in numerous dimensions – they might say it's infinitely more likely.

So I'm open to all this, because the more I became involved in exploring the experiences of ordinary Pembrokeshire people the more frightened I became.

Susan had hoped I would remain unscathed from my proximity to her. Maybe it was just coincidence, maybe not, but while writing up her account I suffered a TIA (a mini-stroke) brought on by a number of hemiplegic migraines, and was eventually diagnosed with bipolar type 2 depression.

Had my closeness to the subjects taken too much of a toll? Had I delved too deep, pushed too hard? I was striving for as complete an account as possible, to present to you, the readers. I put myself under tremendous pressure to do justice to the experiences of my subjects.

Was the supernatural and the strange directly responsible for my ill health? Was I the target of insidious influences? I don't believe so. I believe my ability to cope with stress, the nature of my constitution and psyche were formed by trauma as a child. I cannot and will not blame aliens for my health condition. I chose to take the torch and shine it deep into the darkness. I alone determined which cases to investigate and how hard to pursue the kernels of truth hidden in each mystery, to unravel enigmas to share with the world.

For those confident that these accounts are merely modern fables, fairy tales or horror stories for the gullible, then I am sorry you think that way. I realise that most will think Susan to have been mentally ill, and now I'm doubling down by acknowledging that I have been as well. I've given a lot to these testimonials, much more than a doctor who just prescribes pills. I absorb much negativity from the account and the inevitable backlash that follows. I get ill and depressed after each one. I have documented four accounts in eight years. If I was just interested in writing fiction, I could have written many times that number of horror stories without having had to deal with the sceptical response and being held up for judgement.

This will be my final investigation. I can't stand another ordeal like it. The fear, pain, emotion I absorb from my subjects is too much to bear. I am after all just a man and I want to take root in my own world. A world of light and love, of family and friends. I need to step away from the darkness before I am consumed by it.

What became of Susan?

As the seasons turned into years, I gradually heard less and less from Susan. She had asked that I not publish the testimony until she had finally made her escape from slumbering Pembrokeshire and was off to explore a vibrant beautiful world.

In December 2018 while on a publicity tour for *Haunted: Horror of Haverfordwest* I received an email from her. This is what she wrote:

Dear Gavin,

I hope this email finds you well.

Congratulations on the success of your new book. It seems that there is more to this world than aliens. I have wondered if there is any relation in their origin. There are striking similarities in many paranormal phenomena.

I am sat here at London Heathrow and I am about to embark on my farewell tour.

There is no need to reply, this email was set up just to contact you. Delete it please, once read.

Thank you for everything, for being a friend, for caring, I had forgot what it was like to have someone have a genuine concern for me. It made such a world of difference. It was nice to have a friend again.

Publish the book, make the difference, send the message.

I hope one day to plate up that supper for two.

It was ALL real, Gavin, please know this.

See you on the other side

The loneliest girl in the world

Susan

Reflections

Well, I saw the thing comin' out of the sky
It had the one long horn, one big eye
I commenced to shakin' and I said "ooh-eee"
It looks like a purple people eater to me
Sheb Wooley, *The Purple People Eater*

I didn't want this testimonial to begin and end with just Susan's words. I thought, why not use the Paranormal Chronicles' platforms to do some further research? No one other than myself and Susan, as far as I was concerned, knew about the details of the case. I asked, as part of ongoing research, the people of Pembrokeshire and surrounding areas if anyone had any strange visions, dreams based around aliens or curious UFO sightings. Here is a collection I have permission to publish, anonymously of course.

I think you will be most interested.

I have had a very strange reoccurring dream. I am walking just outside of Clarbeston Road where I live, and I am on my phone talking to my son. It is near dark, it feels like early evening in November or December. As I am walking, I can see an orange light floating just above the Preseli Mountains. It's not the transmission masts, something brighter and bigger. I think it is a plane at first. My son is saying to me he is scared as they have shut the Severn Bridge *(the bridge that connects England and Wales across the River Severn)* and that he can hear explosions in the distance. I am frantically telling him to find another way home. Before I know it, the orange light is above me and I wake up terrified. I must have had this dream about five or six times that I can remember.

I have these crazy dreams that I was walking past the pub in Rosebush near Narberth. There are red lights everywhere, in the sky high above, moving above the trees and hedges. I think they are helicopters but there is no sound at all, just silence. I stand there, beginning to panic as there are hundreds of these lights everywhere. When I wake up, I always think I have seen the beginning of an alien invasion. This is how it will be when it eventually happens.

In my dream I wake up and across the bay (Swansea) where I live, I can see a bright orange light, low on the horizon, I think it must be a ship on fire. I look up and all in the night sky are dozens of these lights flying in formation. I feel so small and paralysed. It feels so real.

I used to work a night shift for a local supermarket and one morning while I was walking home through Merlins Bridge playing field, around 6 or 7, say twenty-five years ago, it was still dark. I saw a bright white light above the fire tower in Haverfordwest. I assumed it was a helicopter as it was silent. I watched it shoot straight up at incredible speed. It was cool to see and not very worrying. I slept in the day and I had an awful dream that someone was in the house with me. Nonsense I think, I'm tired, strange sleep patterns and so on. I woke up to go to the toilet and I was convinced that in the bedroom was an alien, the one with the big eyes, dressed like, well, little red riding hood. It was those big-eyed ones, the one everyone says you're mad if you see, but it had a red hood on, absolutely nuts. I screamed and woke up, but no noise was coming out of me, I couldn't move. I thought I would tell you as I did see that strange light earlier in the day and would love to know if anyone else saw it.

This was something me and some friends saw down Milford

Way, by the golf course late one night. I'm probably going back thirty years. We were walking and we saw silhouetted on the road, these three big rectangular shapes. You could make them out with the lights behind them, they were definitely solid, much taller than us, probably twelve feet, twice the size of us. Anyway, these shapes make this loud screeching noise and started rocking back and forth, in the middle of the road! We just ran as fast as we could in the opposite direction. I don't know was it a prank or not but what a strange thing to set up on a quiet road late at night. They were so loud. Strangest thing ever and never heard of anything like them again.

It was while camping with my family down Newgale around the summer of 2015 that I had a vivid frightening dream that I woke up and outside the tent, hovering right above us, was a huge orange ball of light. It was burning my eyes. I woke up in the morning, exhausted, worried and preoccupied by what I had seen. Later on, in the day, my son, he's only five, complained he was tired, and his mum asked had he not got asleep and he said that the light had kept him and daddy up! I hadn't mentioned it to anyone!! Thankfully it was our last night down there and I didn't have to see what happened the next night.

I dreamt one night, more like a nightmare, that the sky was full of moving stars. I was outside in the cold and I ran inside, and my family were all in the living room talking loudly. My father told everyone to shut up and, on the news, they were talking about the lights. The TV picture was all blocky, like there was interference and the news reporters were saying that the objects had been hiding behind the Sun and were now being spotted all over the world. Instead of the dream just ending I would, I think, flash forward and I would still be at home (Narberth area) and outside all the trees were dead and the sky black. Absolutely terrifying nightmare.

I was living outside of Narberth by the crematorium when I had a strange dream of a glowing white ball in the sky dripping something like molten metal as it passed above my cottage. I woke up the next day and thought very little about my odd little dream. The next night I was putting food in the compost bin and as God is my witness I watched the exact same object from my dream float across the sky and vanish over the hill. I was too confused to be frightened. Every night I lived down there I stood in the garden seeing if I could see it again and take a picture and I never did.

This wasn't a dream, and my daughter and I witnessed it while walking our dog down the Guile *(wooded area with the River Cleddau passing through it)* when our dog stopped walking. She wouldn't move and my daughter and I both witnessed a ball of red light, about the size of a football, shoot up the river. Where it passed it left a wake in the water. We quickly walked back and have never been back there again.

One night I had a vivid dream that there was a bright orange light coming in from the window, brighter than a street light, and in the corner is a tall, so tall, man. He's like a stick, so skinny and it's like he has a motorcycle helmet on, but his neck looks too thin to hold the weight. Many times, I have woken up and I'm staring at the corner of the bedroom. I hate having those feelings that something is there, and I've been talking to someone or something.

I dreamt of a huge shadow passing over Milford Haven. People were looking up too but all you could see was pure blackness. Really strange.

This is less of a dream or sighting, I live in Milford Haven and early one morning, around 3am, my husband found me in the garden. I do sleepwalk. He said I was talking, mumbling, saying could he see the big spaceship floating above the refinery.

I had a wild dream that I was stood outside the hotel on Hamilton Terrace, Milford Haven smoking when I watched a red light shoot up the estuary at a great speed and next thing everything was on fire. I woke up screaming.

Upon wakening from a strange dream, a vision of strange beings and lights in the sky, ask yourself, was it all just a dream? Maybe forces unfathomable to our comprehension are creeping silently into our world and plucking us from our beds like *corn from the field*.

Next time you sit under a full moon and a night full of stars, as you look upon the majestic beauty of the Cosmos, please send a thought of hope to a young woman from Pembrokeshire travelling the world, trying to stay one step ahead of the most unwelcome of visitors. Let's hope they cast their greedy intentions away from her long enough for her to live a fruitful life and maybe even let her find the love and happiness she aches for. We can all hope.

The season of the Harvest is never-ending.

This was her message to the world. Do not let her die in vain.

An Interview with G.L. Davies

January 2019
Long-time collaborator, friend and co-host of The Paranormal Chronicles.com radio show, Dave Dominguez sits down with G.L. Davies to ask him the big questions following on from his fourth book.

Dave Dominguez: Congratulations, Gavin, you have completed your fourth book. I have just finished it and wow, that was terrifying. How does it feel knowing you can step away from it?

G.L. Davies: I feel relieved. It's been a long six years juggling some very demanding and challenging cases. It's been a tough journey but the motivations were to represent the subject, Susan, as accurately as possible and to present it in a way that made sense, her testimony, to the reader. There was a lot of complex imagery and themes to decipher and translate.

The readers are the ones that drive this forward with their theories and exposition. People from all over the world can read this, dissect it, talk about it and branch off with new research, new theories, new approaches, and that is incredibly humbling and satisfying. That is the message Susan is talking about, that the readers will bring her ordeal to life.

You never truly step away from the cases; you are always called back, a radio interview, TV or journalist or even just a reader wanting to reach out to learn more. That is easier to manage I guess, just not so intense as the actual subject interview and the putting it all together.

I owe it to Susan to spread the message and I hope people reading this feel comfortable enough to do so too.

DD: Is it true you suffered a TIA and were diagnosed with bipolar type 2 depression while completing this book?

GLD: I did. It's been an overwhelming six years. I started

2013 as an alcoholic, depressed and in the abyss, and I have used every day since to try and lead a life of meaning. I've been sober for six years. There are some days I find it incredibly difficult to function, in terms of I don't know how I fit into the world, I succumb to my depression and grief, feel very alone; and other days I ride that wave of positivity and embark on as many crazy missions as I can. I like to push myself whenever the fuel is there to succeed. I am blessed that I have the life I have and the people I have in it, you included, Dave. I love them all very much.

DD: Is it healthy to be writing about this subject – dark, worrying, disturbing subjects – if you are prone to depression and, as highlighted in *Haunted: Horror of Haverfordwest*, suicidal tendencies?

GLD: If you are going to have negative and dark thought processes then I imagine the line of work I do is very fitting. People say to me when they read my books, they get a real sense of the paranoia, dread, fear, grief, all the negative aspects, and that is because I am relating to my own experiences, drawing upon my own feelings. It's easy to write about how people are feeling in the grip of depression when you feel that way half your life anyway. Writing about what you know is the key to successful writing.

DD: You have a style named after you, The Davies Style, a paranormal testimonial, almost found-footage style of writing. How did you develop that style?

GLD: *(Laughing)* A style named after me, I don't think so. The style I use is not unique to me at all. I just prefer using it in supernatural accounts. A mentor once told me, modern writing is about finding new ways to tell old stories, to dare to take the risk to do something different. I just wanted to do something different but still compelling.

I had read books written in interview style and they just dragged me in. *World War Z* by Max Brooks was a huge influence. I had read so many books written as a narrative, and I found that the events seemed to be more amplified, sensationalised, and we were missing the real impact of the haunting or event. I want to write about ordinary people's thought processes in extraordinary situations. What were they thinking, what were they feeling, what were they dreaming? Let's paint a three-dimensional picture and the feedback from readers is that they can relate to the interviewees more, they see them as real people, which they are. I don't want these people to be merely characters. They are very real people who have experienced very harrowing episodes and they want their accounts told in an honest fashion.

Some people are turned off by the interview style and I understand this as they are conditioned to read books in a certain way, and it can be quite difficult to reprogram your brain to read something differently. One reviewer really struggled at first but once she got to grips with the style, she said it was like using chopsticks. You have to think about it at first, concentrate on what you are doing, and before you know it you are eating away without thinking.

I hope more fans of the paranormal true account genre adopt this style, evolve it, build upon it and take it to a different level. I would certainly read more books like that. I hope at the very least I inspire people to write.

DD: You wrote in this very book that you were done. Is this true? Is this the last paranormal account from G.L. Davies? Say it ain't so!

GLD: That's it for the accounts, I can't do anymore. This is my fourth in six years and it took over my life. The negativity, the depravity, the helplessness that so many of the people endured, I just absorb it; it leaves me exhausted, ill. Depressed. I am left severely depressed and broken by the experience. I'm 44 this year and I want to settle down, live a little, feel the sun on my face, find my smile. I have someone very special in my life now, and I want to enjoy life.

You have to remember that these people are real. No matter

what the sceptics think, these people are real. I can't say if their accounts are real or not as I'm not the one that has experienced them; well apart from *Haunted: Horror of Haverfordwest*. After months, even years of time spent interviewing them, analysing them, cross-examining them to get to the essence of the testimony, I become very close to these people, and I hate the idea that they are suffering. I feel so helpless. It makes me very ill.

DD: So, you are hanging up your writer's hat?

GLD: Not at all. I've very much explored my dark side, and now I want to explore my bright side. I am a very motivated and passionate person. I genuinely have a desire to see people succeed and achieve, and I want to tap into that, see if I could write about motivational thought processes. Also, after years exploring the horrors of the world, the incomprehensible, I have lots of ideas, images, feelings floating around in my head so I'm going to keep working in the paranormal field. I'm going to explore ghost stories, bring some forgotten ones back to life, maybe create some new terrifying ones. I'll still creep people out some way. I'm just not going to dive into the deep end of long-term interviews and investigations. I have to put myself first. I have sacrificed so much to bring these accounts into the public eye.

DD: You have written about hauntings, dimensional beings, the Spectrophilia (Ghost sex) Phenomenon, and now aliens and alien abduction. Is there one of these subjects that worries you more than the others?

GLD: To be honest, all of them are equally terrifying. To me, it is how the interviewee translates the fear, horror, the confusion that affects me. These are ordinary people, people from beautiful sleepy Pembrokeshire, that feel they are being subjected to a horrific ordeal. Whether these events have psychological explanations or are real, these ordinary people feel they are the victims of something highly negative, powerful and destructive.

The paranormal is not all horror and depressing gloom.

There is so much that is positive, but like everything there is a balance between positive and negative, and I am for some reason drawn to the negative. It may explain my mental health issues, my depressive nature.

I have ventured into the darkness further than most investigators. Some investigators just go to a location for a night with a camera and some techniques, copying what they see on TV. I live the experience; I put my mind into the situation for months, sometimes years. Not many people know this but when I am on my own at night I sleep with the light on.

DD: What's next for you?

GLD: I made a promise to Susan that I would spread the message. I hope wherever she is, she is safe. I hope she finds a sliver of happiness. I hope she is wrong, and it's all over for her. I hope they left her alone.

DD: So, do you believe her?

GLD: I made a promise.

DD: Well I am sure many people will read this book and help spread that message that there may well be something out there that is destroying lives in the most terrifying ways possible. We can only hope Susan is right in that the message will spread, and we can only hope she is safe.

GLD: We will see if she is right that people are too scared to talk about these things because of the pressure from the media, from our scientists, that we are not allowed to believe in such things. It's a sad world if this is all true, and thousands of women, people are losing their lives, and no one is listening. There is no shame in pondering, discussing, talking, researching, and everyone who has read this please just ask yourself, what if? That is a great start. Just talk about this, just say you read a book and it worried you.

Never be afraid to question everything you think you know. We are learning new things every day. Things we thought were fact have been proven differently, and every day we discover something new, we open up a hundred new possibilities. It's highly probable that we are not alone in the universe, and there's an ever-growing mountain of evidence that aliens are visiting our world. If they are here for nefarious reasons, if they are here to hurt us then let's tool up, let's learn, let's expose them, let's see how we can fight back and protect our mothers, fathers, sons and daughters. Let's be prepared. Let's show these beings they can't mess with us anymore; that we won't be taken easily anymore. At the end of the day we have nothing to lose if we are wrong. Let's talk about it openly and let's share Susan's message.

DD: Amen to that. In closing, any final words to the people that read your work?

GLD: Thank you so much, to every one of you who has supported me. Thank you so much. There were times when I didn't think I could hold on anymore, times when I had fallen so far into the abyss, and every kind word, every word of encouragement helped me climb back out and into the sunlight.

I am just a dyslexic man from Pembrokeshire, West Wales, who cares about his interviewees, regardless whether it is real or not. I just wanted to put my heart alongside theirs so the readers can open their minds, explore new worlds, feel the fear, the pain. I want everyone to know that I shone the light into the dark because people should not have to suffer alone or in silence.

To aspiring artists, dancers, singers, writers – follow your heart, follow your passion. Create and build. Feel the beautiful energy of creation, and don't try and fit into the world. Make the world fit into you. Dare to be different, stay strong and talk about how you feel. Never feel inadequate or weak if your brain lets you down and floods you with depression or sadness. Reach out – people do care, they will help you. Never, ever, apologise for feeling happy.

When I was a child I was told I was stupid, and would never amount to anything. Dyslexia and mental health issues weren't widely understood where I grew up. I was locked in cupboards and put in remedial classes. I have faced challenges from every corner imaginable. I've had people try and derail me, criticise me, but tens of thousands of readers, hundreds of investigators and paranormal personalities support my work, my investigations and my writing, and I cannot thank those people enough. It made everything worth it. It's an amazing feeling.

Everyone deserves a chance at life, everyone deserves to be happy. Live, dream, believe and take the bull by the horns.

Thank you so much, everyone, you helped saved my life.

SLEEP WELL

6TH BOOKS

ALL THINGS PARANORMAL

Investigations, explanations and deliberations on the paranormal, supernatural, explainable or unexplainable. 6th Books seeks to give answers while nourishing the soul: whether making use of the scientific model or anecdotal and fun, but always beautifully written.
Titles cover everything within parapsychology: how to, lifestyles, alternative medicine, beliefs, myths and theories.
If you have enjoyed this book, why not tell other readers by posting a review on your preferred book site?

Recent bestsellers from 6th Books are:

The Afterlife Unveiled
What the Dead Are Telling us About Their World!
Stafford Betty
What happens after we die? Spirits speaking through mediums
know, and they want us to know. This book unveils their world...
Paperback: 978-1-84694-496-3 ebook: 978-1-84694-926-5

Spirit Release
Sue Allen
A guide to psychic attack, curses, witchcraft, spirit attachment,
possession, soul retrieval, haunting, deliverance, exorcism and
more, as taught at the College of Psychic Studies.
Paperback: 978-1-84694-033-0 ebook: 978-1-84694-651-6

I'm Still With You
True Stories of Healing Grief Through Spirit Communication
Carole J. Obley
A series of after-death spirit communications which uplift, comfort
and heal, and show how love helps us grieve.
Paperback: 978-1-84694-107-8 ebook: 978-1-84694-639-4

Less Incomplete
A Guide to Experiencing the Human Condition Beyond the
Physical Body
Sandie Gustus
Based on 40 years of scientific research, this book is a dynamic
guide to understanding life beyond the physical body.
Paperback: 978-1-84694-351-5 ebook: 978-1-84694-892-3

Advanced Psychic Development
Becky Walsh
Learn how to practise as a professional, contemporary spiritual medium.
Paperback: 978-1-84694-062-0 ebook: 978-1-78099-941-8

Astral Projection Made Easy
and overcoming the fear of death
Stephanie June Sorrell
From the popular Made Easy series, *Astral Projection Made Easy* helps to eliminate the fear of death, through discussion of life beyond the physical body.
Paperback: 978-1-84694-611-0 ebook: 978-1-78099-225-9

The Miracle Workers Handbook
Seven Levels of Power and Manifestation of the Virgin Mary
Sherrie Dillard
Learn how to invoke the Virgin Mary's presence, communicate with her, receive her grace and miracles and become a miracle worker.
Paperback: 978-1-84694-920-3 ebook: 978-1-84694-921-0

Divine Guidance
The Answers You Need to Make Miracles
Stephanie J. King
Ask any question and the answer will be presented, like a direct line to higher realms… *Divine Guidance* helps you to regain control over your own journey through life.
Paperback: 978-1-78099-794-0 ebook: 978-1-78099-793-3

The End of Death
How Near-Death Experiences Prove the Afterlife
Admir Serrano
A compelling examination of the phenomena of Near-Death
Experiences.
Paperback: 978-1-78279-233-8 ebook: 978-1-78279-232-1

The Psychic & Spiritual Awareness Manual
A Guide to DIY Enlightenment
Kevin West
Discover practical ways of empowering yourself by unlocking
your psychic awareness, through the Spiritualist and New Age
approach.
Paperback: 978-1-78279-397-7 ebook: 978-1-78279-396-0

An Angels' Guide to Working with the Power of Light
Laura Newbury
Discovering her ability to communicate with angels, Laura
Newbury records her inspirational messages of guidance and
answers to universal questions.
Paperback: 978-1-84694-908-1 ebook: 978-1-84694-909-8

The Audible Life Stream
Ancient Secret of Dying While Living
Alistair Conwell
The secret to unlocking your purpose in life is to solve the mystery
of death, while still living.
Paperback: 978-1-84694-329-4 ebook: 978-1-78535-297-3

Beyond Photography
Encounters with Orbs, Angels and Mysterious Light Forms!
John Pickering, Katie Hall
Orbs have been appearing all over the world in recent years. This is the personal account of one couple's experience of this new phenomenon.
Paperback: 978-1-90504-790-1

Blissfully Dead
Life Lessons from the Other Side
Melita Harvey
The spirit of Janelle, a former actress, takes the reader on a fascinating and insightful journey from the mind to the heart.
Paperback: 978-1-78535-078-8 ebook: 978-1-78535-079-5

Does It Rain in Other Dimensions?
A True Story of Alien Encounters
Mike Oram
We have neighbors in the universe. This book describes one man's experience of communicating with other-dimensional and extra-terrestrial beings over a 50-year period.
Paperback: 978-1-84694-054-5

Electronic Voices: Contact with Another Dimension?
Anabela Mourato Cardoso
Career diplomat and experimenter Dr Anabela Cardoso covers the latest research into Instrumental Transcommunication and Electronic Voice Phenomena.
Paperback: 978-1-84694-363-8